OPPOSING VIEWPOINTS® SERIES

Interpreting the Bill of Rights

Other Books of Related Interest

Opposing Viewpoints Series

Identity Politics
Reparations
Voting Rights
Western Democracy at Risk

At Issue Series

The Affordable Care Act
Reproductive Rights
The Right to a Living Wage
When Is Free Speech Hate Speech?

Current Controversies Series

Are There Two Americas?
LGBTQ Rights
Same-Sex Marriage

> "Congress shall make no law … abridging the freedom of speech, or of the press."

First Amendment to the US Constitution

The basic foundation of our democracy is the First Amendment guarantee of freedom of expression. The Opposing Viewpoints series is dedicated to the concept of this basic freedom and the idea that it is more important to practice it than to enshrine it.

Interpreting the Bill
of Rights /
2019.
33305243693144
sa   09/07/18

Interpreting the
Bill of Rights

Avery Elizabeth Hurt, Book Editor

GREENHAVEN
PUBLISHING

Published in 2019 by Greenhaven Publishing, LLC
353 3rd Avenue, Suite 255, New York, NY 10010

Copyright © 2019 by Greenhaven Publishing, LLC

First Edition

Articles in Greenhaven Publishing anthologies are often edited for length to meet page
requirements. In addition, original titles of these works are changed to clearly present
the main thesis and to explicitly indicate the author's opinion. Every effort is made to
ensure that Greenhaven Publishing accurately reflects the original intent of the authors.
Every effort has been made to trace the owners of the copyrighted material.

Cover image: Michael Nagle/Bloomberg via Getty Images

Library of Congress Cataloging-in-Publication Data

Names: Hurt, Avery Elizabeth, editor.
Title: Interpreting the Bill of Rights / Avery Elizabeth Hurt, editor.
Description: New York : Greenhaven Publishing, 2018. | Series: Opposing
  viewpoints | Includes bibliographical references and index. | Audience: Grades 9–12.
Identifiers: LCCN 2017060602| ISBN 9781534502932 (library bound) | ISBN
  9781534502949 (pbk.)
Subjects: LCSH: United States. Constitution. 1st–10th Amendments—Juvenile
  literature. | Civil rights—United States—History—Juvenile literature. |
  Constitutional amendments—United States—History—Juvenile literature.
Classification: LCC KF4750 .I58 2018 | DDC 342.7303—dc23
LC record available at https://lccn.loc.gov/2017060602

Manufactured in the United States of America

Website: http://greenhavenpublishing.com

Contents

Chapter 3: Should Justices Exercise Judicial Restraint in Interpreting the Bill of Rights?

Chapter 4: Has the Court Become Too Political in Interpreting the Bill of Rights?

The Importance of Opposing Viewpoints

Perhaps every generation experiences a period in time in which the populace seems especially polarized, starkly divided on the important issues of the day and gravitating toward the far ends of the political spectrum and away from a consensus-facilitating middle ground. The world that today's students are growing up in and that they will soon enter into as active and engaged citizens is deeply fragmented in just this way. Issues relating to terrorism, immigration, women's rights, minority rights, race relations, health care, taxation, wealth and poverty, the environment, policing, military intervention, the proper role of government—in some ways, perennial issues that are freshly and uniquely urgent and vital with each new generation—are currently roiling the world.

If we are to foster a knowledgeable, responsible, active, and engaged citizenry among today's youth, we must provide them with the intellectual, interpretive, and critical-thinking tools and experience necessary to make sense of the world around them and of the all-important debates and arguments that inform it. After all, the outcome of these debates will in large measure determine the future course, prospects, and outcomes of the world and its peoples, particularly its youth. If they are to become successful members of society and productive and informed citizens, students need to learn how to evaluate the strengths and weaknesses of someone else's arguments, how to sift fact from opinion and fallacy, and how to test the relative merits and validity of their own opinions against the known facts and the best possible available information. The landmark series Opposing Viewpoints has been providing students with just such critical-thinking skills and exposure to the debates surrounding society's most urgent contemporary issues for many years, and it continues to serve this essential role with undiminished commitment, care, and rigor.

The key to the series's success in achieving its goal of sharpening students' critical-thinking and analytic skills resides in its title—

Opposing Viewpoints. In every intriguing, compelling, and engaging volume of this series, readers are presented with the widest possible spectrum of distinct viewpoints, expert opinions, and informed argumentation and commentary, supplied by some of today's leading academics, thinkers, analysts, politicians, policy makers, economists, activists, change agents, and advocates. Every opinion and argument anthologized here is presented objectively and accorded respect. There is no editorializing in any introductory text or in the arrangement and order of the pieces. No piece is included as a "straw man," an easy ideological target for cheap point-scoring. As wide and inclusive a range of viewpoints as possible is offered, with no privileging of one particular political ideology or cultural perspective over another. It is left to each individual reader to evaluate the relative merits of each argument— as he or she sees it, and with the use of ever-growing critical-thinking skills—and grapple with his or her own assumptions, beliefs, and perspectives to determine how convincing or successful any given argument is and how the reader's own stance on the issue may be modified or altered in response to it.

This process is facilitated and supported by volume, chapter, and selection introductions that provide readers with the essential context they need to begin engaging with the spotlighted issues, with the debates surrounding them, and with their own perhaps shifting or nascent opinions on them. In addition, guided reading and discussion questions encourage readers to determine the authors' point of view and purpose, interrogate and analyze the various arguments and their rhetoric and structure, evaluate the arguments' strengths and weaknesses, test their claims against available facts and evidence, judge the validity of the reasoning, and bring into clearer, sharper focus the reader's own beliefs and conclusions and how they may differ from or align with those in the collection or those of their classmates.

Research has shown that reading comprehension skills improve dramatically when students are provided with compelling, intriguing, and relevant "discussable" texts. The subject matter of these collections could not be more compelling, intriguing, or urgently relevant to today's students and the world they are poised to inherit. The anthologized articles and the reading and discussion questions that are included with them also provide the basis for stimulating, lively, and passionate classroom debates. Students who are compelled to anticipate objections to their own argument and identify the flaws in those of an opponent read more carefully, think more critically, and steep themselves in relevant context, facts, and information more thoroughly. In short, using discussable text of the kind provided by every single volume in the Opposing Viewpoints series encourages close reading, facilitates reading comprehension, fosters research, strengthens critical thinking, and greatly enlivens and energizes classroom discussion and participation. The entire learning process is deepened, extended, and strengthened.

For all of these reasons, Opposing Viewpoints continues to be exactly the right resource at exactly the right time—when we most need to provide readers with the critical-thinking tools and skills that will not only serve them well in school but also in their careers and their daily lives as decision-making family members, community members, and citizens. This series encourages respectful engagement with and analysis of opposing viewpoints and fosters a resulting increase in the strength and rigor of one's own opinions and stances. As such, it helps make readers "future ready," and that readiness will pay rich dividends for the readers themselves, for the citizenry, for our society, and for the world at large.

Introduction

> *Given the complicated balance*
> *between an individual's rights and*
> *society's needs—between liberty and*
> *security—we will be debating the Bill*
> *of Rights for as long as we have one*
> *to debate.*
>
> Andrew Rudalevige
> Washington Post

Controversies about the US Bill of Rights are nothing new. One of the first major debates of the new nation was over whether or not to even have one.

After the American colonists won the Revolutionary War, they faced a task just as formidable, if not as bloody. If the thirteen separate, and in many ways disparate, colonies were to become a nation, they would need a framework for their government, a user's manual of sorts that would spell out exactly how the new nation would be governed. In the summer of 1787, delegates from each of the thirteen colonies gathered in Philadelphia to take on this task. The first draft of the remarkable document that became the Constitution of the United States of America organized the government into three equal but delicately balanced branches. It spelled out how leaders were to be elected and how the judiciary was to be organized. It was quite specific about what the new federal government could do and how it was to go about doing it. It was mainly silent, however, on what that government could not do. This omission was a serious problem. For many it was a nonstarter. The colonies had just fought a bloody war to throw off what they considered an oppressive government. They weren't about to sign on the dotted line for another government without some guarantees that their hard-won liberties would be protected.

The solution was to include a Bill of Rights. Though today we may argue over details of what exactly these rights mean and how they should be protected, we consider these first ten amendments so fundamental to our government and society that some have called them the Constitution's Ten Commandments. However, it was not always thus—at least not among the delegates in charge of drafting the constitution.

There were several reasons most of the delegates initially opposed a bill of rights. Some feared that spelling out specific rights would imply that those were the only guaranteed rights. (The last two amendments took care of this problem.) Others simply thought it was unnecessary, that the federal government would not be powerful enough to deny citizens their rights. In any case, many states already had similar sets of rights spelled out in their constitutions, so wasn't a federal bill of rights redundant? Some of the founders feared that a bill of rights would weaken the power of the central government—tipping the balance of power from the government to the people. This, of course, was the point. The people were demanding very specific protections from their new government. Without them, it was unlikely that the Constitution would be ratified by enough of the states to form a functional government.

In the end, those in favor of a list of rights won the day. James Madison, who had been the primary author of the Constitution, drafted a set of amendments to the new Constitution. He came up with nineteen, which were whittled down to twelve rather quickly. The first two were then scrapped as well, and the final ten were ratified and became a part of the US Constitution on December 15, 1791.

While this ended the debate about whether there should be a Bill of Rights, it began a series of new debates about how those rights should be interpreted, how they should be defended, and whose responsibility it is to protect them. In answering these questions, Americans are called upon to decide just what the Bill of Rights—and more broadly the Constitution—really is. And, of course, that means deciding who we are as a nation, what our values and priorities are.

In *Opposing Viewpoints: Interpreting the Bill of Rights*, you will read the thoughts of people who have spent much time debating these issues. In chapters titled Why Do We Need a Bill of Rights?, How Should We Interpret the Bill of Rights?, Should Justices Exercise Judicial Restraint in Interpreting the Bill of Rights?, and Has the Court Become Too Political in Interpreting the Bill of Rights?, viewpoint authors explore the complex issues inherent in applying words written hundreds of years ago to today's society. They approach the topic from a variety of political and philosophical perspectives, but they all have one thing in common: they deeply respect the Bill of Rights and the nation it protects.

OPPOSING
VIEWPOINTS®
SERIES

CHAPTER 1

Why Do We Need a Bill of Rights?

Chapter Preface

Almost as soon as the ink was dry on the US Constitution, some people began to demand that it be amended to contain a bill of rights. Today, it's hard to imagine the idea as even remotely controversial. The Bill of Rights is the part of the Constitution modern Americans are most familiar with—and it's the part that we most revere. However it was a surprisingly hard sell. Most of the framers of the Constitution feared a bill of rights would limit the federal government too much and weaken the bonds among the states. Meanwhile, many of the people who would have to ratify the Constitution believed that without a bill of rights, individual rights would not be adequately protected. As you will see in the following viewpoints, the arguments for and against a bill of rights were quite nuanced. In the end, it was necessary to include a bill of rights to garner enough support for ratification of the Constitution.

That did not stop the arguments, however. Questions and controversies soon emerged about to whom these rights applied and how they were best enforced. As you will see in the following viewpoints, uniting a group of independent-minded and often fractious colonists into a well-organized and cooperative nation took more than getting everyone to sign on to the blueprint for running the federal government. Even after the Constitution was ratified, arguments about who had what power and how much still needed to be addressed. It would take almost another century and a devastating civil war before the United States truly became one nation.

The first few viewpoints here outline the rights themselves before discussing the debates about their ratification. The first, in particular, carefully identifies which rights are protected by each amendment—something that can be a bit difficult nowadays owing to the old-fashioned language of the document. Then you will read about who was left out of the Bill of Rights, and why that was a disaster waiting to happen.

> "*The Bill of Rights remains an active force in contemporary American life as a major element of Constitutional Law. The meaning of its protections remains hotly debated.*"

The Demand for a Bill of Rights

USHistory.org

In the following viewpoint, the authors from the website USHistory .org present highlights of the history of the Bill of Rights, as well as a complete list of the amendments themselves. The inclusion of a Bill of Rights was not without debate, and the viewpoint authors preview some of the issues that will be discussed later in the chapter and throughout this resource. The language of the amendments can be confusing, and the viewpoint helpfully lists which specific rights are protected by each of the first ten amendments.

As you read, consider the following questions:

1. What were the fears and concerns of the crucial states of Massachusetts, Virginia, and New York?
2. What statement of rights does the government of England have?
3. Why do you think James Madison was chosen to draft the Bill of Rights?

The first national election occurred in 1789. Along with President Washington, voters elected a large number of supporters of the Constitution. In fact, almost half of the ninety-one members of the first Congress had helped to write or ratify the Constitution.

Not surprisingly, given Anti-Federalists' opposition to the strong new central government, only eight opponents of the Constitution were sent to the House of Representatives. Most Anti-Federalists concentrated their efforts in state politics.

Protection of Individual Rights

An immediate issue that the new Congress took up was how to modify the Constitution. Representatives were responding to calls for amendments that had emerged as a chief issue during the ratification process. Crucial states of Massachusetts, Virginia, and New York (among others) had all ultimately supported the Constitution—but only with the expectation that explicit protections for individual rights would be added to the highest law of the land. Now that supporters of the Constitution controlled the federal government, what would they do?

The legal tradition of having a precise statement of individual rights had deep roots in Anglo-American custom. So it's not surprising that the first Congress amended the Constitution by adding what became known as the Bill of Rights.

James Madison, now a member of Congress from Virginia, once again took the leading role crafting proposed amendments that would be sent to the states for approval. Madison skillfully reviewed numerous proposals and examples from state constitutions and ultimately selected nineteen potential amendments to the Constitution.

As one might expect, the nationalist Madison took care to make sure that none of the proposed amendments would fundamentally weaken the new central government. In the end, ten amendments were ratified in 1791.

Ten Amendments

These first ten amendments to the Constitution became known as the Bill of Rights and still stand as both the symbol and foundation of American ideals of individual liberty, Limited Government, and the rule of law. Most of the Bill of Rights concerns legal protections for those accused of crimes.

Rights and Protections Guaranteed in the Bill of Rights

AMENDMENT	RIGHTS AND PROTECTIONS
First	Freedom of speech Freedom of the press Freedom of religion Freedom of assembly Right to petition the government
Second	Right to bear arms
Third	Protection against housing soldiers in civilian homes
Fourth	Protection against unreasonable search and seizure Protection against the issuing of warrants without probable cause
Fifth	Protection against: trial without indictment double jeopardy self-incrimination property seizure
Sixth	Right to a speedy trial Right to be informed of charges Right to be confronted by witnesses Right to call witnesses Right to a legal counsel
Seventh	Right to trial by jury
Eighth	Protection against: excessive bail excessive fines cruel and unusual punishment
Ninth	Rights granted in the Constitution shall not infringe on other rights.
Tenth	Powers not granted to the Federal Government in the Constitution belong to the states or the people.

For instance, the fourth through eighth amendments provide protection from unreasonable Search and Seizure, the privilege against Self-Incrimination, and the right to a Fair and Speedy Jury Trial that will be free from unusual punishments.

The First Amendment, perhaps the broadest and most famous of the Bill of Rights, establishes a range of political and civil rights including those of Free Speech, assembly, press, and religion.

The last two amendments, respectively, spell out that this list of individual protections is not meant to exclude other ones, and, by contrast, set forth that all powers claimed by the federal government had to be expressly stated in the Constitution.

The Full Text of the Bill of Rights

Amendment I Congress shall make no law respecting an establishment of religion, or prohibiting the free exercise thereof; or abridging the freedom of speech, or of the press; or the right of the people peaceably to assemble, and to petition the Government for a redress of grievances.

Amendment II A well regulated Militia, being necessary to the security of a free State, the right of the people to keep and bear Arms, shall not be infringed.

Amendment III No Soldier shall, in time of peace be quartered in any house, without the consent of the Owner, nor in time of war, but in a manner to be prescribed by law.

Amendment IV The right of the people to be secure in their persons, houses, papers, and effects, against unreasonable searches and seizures, shall not be violated, and no Warrants shall issue, but upon probable cause, supported by Oath or affirmation, and particularly describing the place to be searched, and the persons or things to be seized.

Amendment V No person shall be held to answer for a capital, or otherwise infamous crime, unless on a presentment or indictment of a Grand Jury, except in cases arising in the land or naval forces, or in the Militia, when in actual service in time of War or public danger; nor shall any person be subject for the same offence to be twice put in jeopardy of life or limb; nor shall be compelled in any criminal case to be a witness against himself, nor be deprived of life, liberty, or property, without due process of law; nor shall private property be taken for public use, without just compensation.

Amendment VI In all criminal prosecutions, the accused shall enjoy the right to a speedy and public trial, by an impartial jury of the State and district wherein the crime shall have been committed, which district shall have been previously ascertained by law, and to be informed of the nature and cause of the accusation; to be confronted with the witnesses against him; to have compulsory process for obtaining witnesses in his favor, and to have the Assistance of Counsel for his defense.

Amendment VII In suits at common law, where the value in controversy shall exceed twenty dollars, the right of trial by jury shall be preserved, and no fact tried by a jury, shall be otherwise reexamined in any Court of the United States, than according to the rules of the common law.

Amendment VIII Excessive bail shall not be required, nor excessive fines imposed, nor cruel and unusual punishments inflicted.

Amendment IX The enumeration in the Constitution, of certain rights, shall not be construed to deny or disparage others retained by the people.

Amendment X The powers not delegated to the United States by the Constitution, nor prohibited by it to the States, are reserved to the States respectively, or to the people.

While the Bill of Rights created no deep challenge to federal authority, it did respond to the central Anti-Federalist fear that the Constitution would unleash an oppressive central government too distant from the people to be controlled.

By responding to this opposition and following through on the broadly expressed desire for amendments that emerged during the ratification process, the Bill of Rights helped to secure broad political support for the new national government. A first major domestic issue had been successfully resolved.

Understanding the Bill of Rights

The Bill of Rights remains an active force in contemporary American life as a major element of Constitutional Law. The meaning of its protections remains hotly debated. For example, the privilege to bear arms to support a militia, which appears in the second amendment, produces significant political controversy today.

More sweepingly, the extension of the Bill of Rights to protect individuals from abuse not only by the federal government, but also from state and local governments remains an unsettled aspect of Constitutional interpretation.

Originally, the protections were solely meant to limit the federal government, but with the fourteenth amendment's guarantee in 1868 that no state could deprive its citizens of the protections in the Bill of Rights this original view began to be expanded. To this day the Supreme Court has not definitively decided if the entire Bill of Rights should always be applied to all levels of government.

> "The Constitution was, as one commentator has said, 'a bundle of compromises' that was designed to meet certain specific needs and to remedy the defects experienced under the Articles of Confederation."

Ratification Required a Bundle of Compromises

Constitutional Rights Foundation

In the following viewpoint, authors from the Constitutional Rights Foundation explore the framing of the US Constitution and the process that lead to its ratification and the inclusion of a bill of rights. The viewpoint authors present direct quotes from the founders as they debated this important issue. Notice how real-life issues, such as war debt and the relationships among the individual states, affected the decisions made by the delegates. The Constitutional Rights Foundation educates American youth about the Constitution and Bill of Rights.

Reprinted with permission, Bill of Rights in Action, 25(2),2009. Retrieved from http://www.crf-usa.org/bill-of-rights-in-action/bria-25-2-the-major-debates-at-the-constitutional-convention.html (Constitutional Rights Foundation).

As you read, consider the following questions:

1. Why was representation such a contentious issue, and what did this have to do with the eventual inclusion of a bill of rights?

2. Why did the delegates who were opposed to slavery give in to the slaveholding states?

3. What are some of the "unforeseen consequences" of the compromises alluded to in this viewpoint?

In 1781 in the midst of the Revolutionary War, the 13 states had agreed to establish a new central government under the Articles of Confederation and Perpetual Union. The Articles created a confederation of states: Each state retained "its sovereignty, freedom, and independence." The weak central government consisted of Congress, a single house in which each state had only one vote. No other branch of government existed: no executive or judiciary. And the Congress had no power to regulate trade or to levy and collect taxes.

By 1787, debts from the Revolutionary War were piling up, and many states had fallen behind in paying what they owed. States were imposing tariffs on each other and fighting over borders. Britain was angry because pre-war debts were not being paid, and it was refusing to honor the treaty that had ended the war (the Paris Treaty of 1783). Recognizing that things were not going well, Congress declared, on February 21, 1787, "that there are defects in the present Confederation" and resolved that a convention should be held in Philadelphia "for the sole and express purpose of revising the Articles of Confederation . . . and to render the Federal Constitution adequate to the exigencies of Government and the preservation of the Union."

On May 25, the convention went into session at the Philadelphia statehouse. George Washington was elected the presiding officer. The delegates quickly decided that their discussions should not be made public and that "nothing spoken in the House be printed, or otherwise published or communicated." Because of the secrecy rule, the public knew little of what was happening inside the Philadelphia statehouse. And without the careful notes taken by James Madison, who attended every session and carefully transcribed the proceedings, today we would know little about how the Constitution came into being.

Before the convention officially began, Madison and the other delegates from Virginia had drafted a plan—the Virginia Plan—for correcting the Articles of Confederation. Their plan went well beyond amendments and corrections and actually laid out a completely new instrument of government. The plan provided for three separate branches of government: legislative, executive, and judicial. The legislative branch would have two houses, with the first house to be elected by the people of each state, and the second by the first house from a list created by the state legislatures.

Representation in Congress

The general outline of the Virginia plan was well received. But the question arose over how to elect the members of the two houses of Congress. For half the summer, the convention debated this issue. Some delegates strongly opposed having the people elect the lower house. Roger Sherman of Connecticut distrusted the notion of democracy. People, he said, "should have as little to do as may be about government" because they are "constantly liable to be misled." Others spoke strongly in favor of popular vote, including George Mason of Virginia. Mason had faith in the common man and believed that the members of the lower house "ought to know and sympathize with every part of the community."

The most difficult issue, however, was the question of how the states were to be represented in Congress. Should all the states have the same number of votes (as they did under the Articles of Confederation where each state had one vote)? Or should each state's number of votes depend on the size of its population (or wealth) as proposed in the Virginia plan? This issue blocked the proceedings for many weeks. Representatives from small states believed that representation based on population would destroy their state's rights. David Brearley of New Jersey said that representation based on population was unfair and unjust. "The large states," he said, "will carry everything before them," and the small states, like Georgia, "will be obliged to throw themselves constantly into the scale of some large one in order to have any weight at all." Other delegates, like James Wilson of Pennsylvania, (one of the three big states), argued that only representation based on population would be fair: For New Jersey, a state with about a third of the population of Pennsylvania, to have the same number of votes as Pennsylvania, "I say no! It is unjust."

On June 30, the delegates from Connecticut proposed a compromise. According to Madison's notes, they suggested that "the proportion of suffrage in the 1st branch should be according to the number of free inhabitants; and that in the second branch or senate, each state should have one vote and no more." The proposal did not stop the bitter opposition and fierce debate. Some delegates began to leave in protest, and a sense of gloom settled over the statehouse. "It seems," Sherman said, "that we have got to a point that we cannot move one way or another." Washington wrote to Alexander Hamilton (who was away) that the crisis was so bad that he almost despaired of seeing a favorable outcome.

Intense debates lasted for two more weeks. Finally, the delegates came together and on July 16 agreed to the Connecticut compromise.

Representation in the lower house would be chosen by the people. The number of each state's representatives would be based on the state's total white population plus three fifths of its slave population. Each state would have one representative for every 40,000 inhabitants (later changed to one for every 30,000). Also each state would have at least one representative even if it did not have 40,000 inhabitants.

Each state would have two members in the Senate, chosen by the state legislature. The small states were jubilant, and the large states uncomfortable. But from then on, things moved more smoothly.

Giving Power to the President

After arriving at a compromise on electing the legislature, the convention addressed the other parts of the Virginia Plan. The plan called for a national executive but did not say how long the executive should serve. The executive would have "a general authority to execute the national laws." The plan also resolved that the executive, working with a committee of judges, should have the power to review and veto laws passed by the Congress, "unless the act of the National Legislature be again passed."

The delegates generally agreed on the need for a separate executive independent of the legislature. (The executive would be called the "president.") And they also agreed on giving the president the power to veto laws but only if his veto was subject to an override. As Madison noted:

> Mr. Sherman was against enabling any one man to stop the will of the whole. No man could be found so far above all the rest in wisdom.

They came to a quick decision that the executive should have the power to veto legislation subject to a two-thirds override in both houses of the legislature. But they could not easily agree on how the executive should be elected.

Delegates proposed many different methods for electing the president. One alternative was direct election by the people, but this drew controversy. Some delegates did not trust the judgment of the common man. Others thought it was simply impractical in a country with many rural communities spread out over a huge area. George Mason of Virginia said:

> . . . it would be as unnatural to refer the choice of a proper character for Chief Magistrate to the people, as it would be to refer a trial of colours to a blind man. The extent of the Country renders it impossible that the people can have the requisite capacity to judge of the respective pretensions of the Candidates.

Another alternative was to have the president chosen, either by the national or state legislatures. Some believed that an executive

No Bill of Rights, No Constitution

Thomas Jefferson argued that "When governments fear the people, there is liberty. When the people fear the government, there is tyranny. The strongest reason for the people to retain the right to keep and bear arms is, as a last resort, to protect themselves against tyranny in government." To me, this important quote (from his Monticello Papers) sets the stage for the ideas behind the Bill of Rights, which are the first ten amendments of the US Constitution.

These amendments were not an afterthought to make the Constitution better, but became a line in the sand in the eyes of those who feared that government did not have sufficient limits placed on it in then newly developed Constitution. The events that led to their inclusion were driven by Virginia delegate George Mason. Simply put, without the ratification of the Bill of Rights, there would be no ratification of the Constitution.

"Bill of Rights Were Designed to Protect the People, Not the Government," by Kevin Price, ©Kevin Price, January 22, 2011.

chosen by the national legislature would be a "mere creature" of the legislature without independent judgment.

Delegates voted more than 60 times before the method was chosen. The final agreement was to have the president elected by electors in each state who would be chosen "in such manner" as its legislature might "direct." Each elector would vote for two people (one of whom could not be an inhabitant of the same state.) The person with the most votes would become president. But if no person had a majority of the votes, the House of Representatives would choose the candidate from the top five (with each state's delegation casting one vote.)

Two more questions about the president also provoked intense debate: How long should the president's term be? And should limits be placed on the number of terms the president could serve? Underlying this debate was a fear of a monarchy, or of a despot, taking over the country. The convention finally decided on a four-year term, with no limit on how many times the president could be re-elected.

Stopping the Slave Trade

A deep disagreement arose over slavery. The economy of many of the Southern states depended almost entirely on agricultural products produced by slaves. To protect their economy, the Southern states insisted on two proposals. One was to ban Congress from taxing exports (to protect their agricultural exports). The second proposal was to forbid Congress from banning the importation of slaves. (In fact, the word "slave" was never used in the Constitution. The proposal was written to prohibit Congress from interfering with the importation "of such persons" as the states "shall think proper to admit.")

When the convention received the draft containing these proposals, another heated debate erupted. Opponents of the ban on exports objected on economic grounds. One delegate said that denying the power to tax exports would take away from the government "half of the regulation of trade." Another pointed out that taxing exports could become important "when America should become a manufacturing country."

Those opposed to slavery brought up issues of morality. Luther Martin of Maryland said that forbidding Congress from banning the importation of slaves was "inconsistent with the principles of the revolution and dishonorable to the American character." Gouverneur Morris of Pennsylvania said that slavery was a "nefarious institution" and a "curse of heaven on the states where it prevailed." George Mason of Virginia spoke at length about the horrors of slavery and criticized slave owners, who he called "petty tyrants," and the slave traders who, he said, "from a lust of gain embarked on this nefarious traffic."

Ultimately, the delegates who strongly opposed slavery realized that pressing against it would make it impossible for the states to come together. They worked out a compromise with the Southern states. They agreed that Congress could not tax exports and that no law could be passed to ban the slave trade until 1808. And in a final concession to the South, the delegates approved a fugitive slave clause. It required that any person "held to Service of Labour in one State" who escapes into another state "shall be delivered up on Claim of the Party to whom such Service or Labour may be due." (The requirement to return fugitive slaves was eliminated when the 13th Amendment abolished slavery.)

Why No Bill of Rights?

The delegates had been meeting for almost four months when the Committee of Style presented a final draft of the Constitution on September 12. The draft contained a new provision, requiring trial by jury in criminal cases tried in the new federal court system. Trial by jury was considered one of many basic rights, and George Mason stood up and proposed including a full bill of rights, listing the basic individual rights that the government could not violate. He believed a bill of rights would "give great quiet to the people" and could be written up in just a few hours. Eldridge Gerry agreed and moved for a committee to prepare a bill of rights. Mason seconded his motion, but it was defeated, by a vote of 10 to 0. (Each state had one vote, and only 10 states were represented for that vote.)

It is not clear why the motion failed. Eight states already had constitutions that included a bill of rights, so one might have been drafted quickly. But Madison's notes don't explain the motion's defeat. He quotes only the words of Roger Sherman who said that "the State Declarations of Rights are not repealed by this Constitution and, being in force, are sufficient.

Three months after the Constitution was signed, Thomas Jefferson wrote to Madison saying that it had been a big mistake to omit a bill of rights. "A bill of rights," he said, "is what the people are entitled to against every government on earth." And many others agreed. When the Constitution was being ratified by the states, many people opposed the Constitution just because it did not contain a bill of rights. In Massachusetts, and in six other states, the ratifying conventions recommended adding a bill of rights to the Constitution. And soon after the first Congress convened in 1789, it responded to the request of the seven states and approved 10 constitutional amendments (drafted by James Madison) that became the Bill of Rights.

'Tis Done

On Monday, September 17, when the delegates met to sign the Constitution, Benjamin Franklin had prepared a speech. The Constitution may not be perfect, he said, but "I cannot help expressing a wish that every member of the Convention who may still have objections to it . . . to make manifest our unanimity, put his name to this instrument." And all of the 44 delegates who were present did sign except for three, including Eldridge Gerry of Massachusetts, who said that he feared "civil war" in his home state and wished that the plan had been put together "in a more mediating shape, in order to abate the heat and opposition of the parties." The work was finished at 4 o'clock when, according to George Washington's diary, the "members adjourned to the City Tavern, dined together and took a cordial leave of each other."

When the document was presented to Congress and to the country, it surprised everyone. In fact, it provoked controversy in many states. But by July 1788, nine states had ratified it, and it went into effect. Elections were held, and on March 4, 1789, the first Congress and president, George Washington, took office under the new US Constitution.

The Constitution was, as one commentator has said, "a bundle of compromises" that was designed to meet certain specific needs and to remedy the defects experienced under the Articles of Confederation. Compromises had been necessary at every point, and in some cases produced unforeseen results. But the Constitution succeeded beyond even the hopes of its strongest advocates. As Benjamin Rush wrote, after a celebration in Philadelphia: "'Tis done. We have become a nation."

> *"Implicit in the story surrounding our Bill of Rights is the proposition that the liberties of a nation can only be secured by citizens of firm conviction who understand our rights and liberties and will actively defend them."*

Having a Bill of Rights Requires That Citizens Understand and Defend Those Rights

Joseph Postell

In the following viewpoint, Joseph Postell begins with a call for citizens to understand and defend the rights guaranteed them by the Bill of Rights. The author goes on to discuss in more detail the debates about including a Bill of Rights, and closes with a powerful argument that the very existence of a Bill of Rights demands that citizens learn about and defend their constitutional rights, and that such a directive is included in the document itself. Joseph Postell is a professor of political science at the University of Colorado at Colorado Springs, and a fellow at the Heritage Foundation.

"Securing Liberty: The Purpose and Importance of the Bill of Rights," by Joseph Postell, The Heritage Foundation, December 14, 2007. Reprinted by permission.

As you read, consider the following questions:

1. Why were Federalists opposed to the Bill of Rights—even if one might have increased chances of ratification by Anti-Federalists?
2. Why did James Madison ultimately change his mind about the Bill of Rights?
3. With whom did Madison believe the safeguard of individual liberty must lie?

National Bill of Rights Day customarily occupies a minor place on our calendars, if it occupies a place at all. It falls every year on December 15, commemorating the ratification of the first 10 amendments to our Constitution, which occurred on that day in 1791. Bill of Rights Day is a day for rising above the commotion over the meaning of each specific amendment. It is an opportunity for us to reflect upon the purpose of those amendments as a whole, to step back and consider the crucial questions that our Founders confronted in considering the idea of amending the Constitution to include a bill of rights.

Implicit in the story surrounding our Bill of Rights is the proposition that the liberties of a nation can only be secured by citizens of firm conviction who understand our rights and liberties and will actively defend them. As Americans studying this important document, we revivify in the public mind the rights and privileges set forth in these amendments. And in doing so, we dutifully fulfill its original purpose.

Parchment Barriers

Although the Founders had extensive experience with bills of rights in the various states, at the Constitutional Convention there was little support for, or even discussion of, placing a statement resembling a bill of rights in the Constitution. When two of the Convention's most influential delegates, Elbridge Gerry and George Mason, proposed adding a bill of rights to the Constitution, their proposal was rejected by a unanimous vote of the states after receiving very little discussion.

The story of the Bill of Rights can be told as the story of how and why the Convention did not support a bill of rights and how James Madison, the "Father of the Constitution," was persuaded to take on the duty of serving as the "Father of the Bill of Rights" in the First Congress.

The Founders' indifference toward a bill of rights in the national Constitution was premised on the idea that it would not be practically useful. The experience of the states in the 1780s demonstrated that bills of rights, though suitable for theoretical treatises, imposed no effective restraints on those who would be responsible for protecting rights in practice. As Alexander Hamilton wrote in Federalist 84, the provisions of the various state bills of rights "would sound much better in a treatise of ethics than in a constitution of government." Benjamin Rush similarly stated that those states which had tried to secure their liberties with a bill of rights had "encumbered their constitutions with that idle and superfluous instrument." The Founders at the Convention believed that a bill of rights would be merely another "parchment barrier" incapable of restraining those who would seek to violate its provisions, and thus it would fail to provide true security for liberty.

The Federalists' Opposition to a Bill of Rights

The indifference of the Federalists—the defenders of the proposed Constitution—to a bill of rights turned into outright opposition when the Anti-Federalists denounced the Constitution and sought to obstruct its ratification. Near or at the top of most Anti-Federalists' lists of objections to the Constitution was the absence of a bill of rights. In response to this opposition, the Federalists argued that a bill of rights would be "not only unnecessary in the proposed constitution, but would even be dangerous."[3] Their arguments are worth considering for what they teach us about the central principles of our Constitution.

First and most importantly, the defenders of the Constitution argued that a bill of rights would undermine the idea of a government with limited powers. A bill of rights might betray the central principle of a written constitution as the product of a social compact, which affirms that all authority originally resides in the people and that the people create a government of limited and enumerated powers in a written constitution.

To suggest, for example, that the liberty of the press is not to be infringed upon might imply that, without such a provision, the federal government would possess that power. The Founders feared that we might infer that they created a government with unlimited power and that the specific provisions in the Bill of Rights denote particular reservations of power from an otherwise unlimited government. James Wilson made this argument most forcefully in speeches defending the Constitution in the state of Pennsylvania. The theory underlying the Constitution, he argued, is that "congressional power is to be collected, not from tacit implications, but from the positive grant expressed in the instrument of the union. Hence…everything which is not given is reserved." Therefore, the presence of a bill of rights "would have supposed that we were throwing into the general government every power not expressly reserved by the people." Similarly, Alexander Hamilton contended that a bill of rights "would contain various exceptions to powers which are not granted; and on this very account, would afford a colourable pretext to claim more than were granted. For why declare that things shall not be done which there is no power to do?"

Adding to this first difficulty was a second problem: A bill of rights, Federalists argued, could not sufficiently define the rights that individuals possess by nature and those rights and privileges which governments are obliged to secure to citizens. Thus, a bill of rights would not only "afford a colourable pretext" for the government to claim more power than was granted to it by the Constitution; it would also insufficiently enumerate the rights which ought to be protected by the government. This would imply that any right not explicitly mentioned in the Bill of Rights must not be protected by it. Due to the impossibility of defining all of the rights which government must respect, a bill of rights would leave a window open for government to infringe upon the rights of its citizens. The centuries-old history of American constitutional law serves to illustrate the force of this argument. Even the greatest American jurists disagreed about the meaning of the provisions of these amendments.

Federalists advanced a third and more subtle critique, namely that a bill of rights might confuse people about the ultimate source of their rights. Many Federalists thought there was no need for a declaration of rights in 1787, because the work had already been done in 1776. In the Declaration of Independence, our Founders had declared that all human beings are endowed with natural and inalienable rights by virtue of their participation in the same fundamental human nature. What need was there to set forth these principles again, particularly in a document whose purpose was not to describe the natural state of man but to establish the institutional framework of the government? To declare our fundamental rights in a document subject to ratification by the people suggested a dangerous principle, namely that the source of rights lies in consent and agreement rather than nature. In other words, a bill of rights might suggest to the people that their rights come from positive law, agreement, and judicial enforcement rather than nature. As Jack Rakove writes, "By implying that traditional rights and liberties would be rendered insecure if they went undeclared, Anti-Federalists in effect suggested that the existence of these rights depended upon their positive expression."

Madison's Change of Opinion

Ultimately, James Madison and most of the other Federalists changed their minds and favored ratification of the amendments we today call our Bill of Rights. While many historical accounts suggest that Madison and the Federalists acquiesced in the adoption of these amendments because it was the only pathway to ratification of the Constitution, they did not change their position due to mere political opportunism. As Rakove points out, "Contrary to the usual story, the concessions that Federalist leaders offered to secure ratification in such closely divided states as Massachusetts, Virginia, and New York did not establish a binding contract to provide a bill of rights." In fact, by the time the First Congress met in April of 1789, the necessity of appeasing the Anti-Federalists on this point had subsided. Thus, the existence of the first 10 amendments to the Constitution cannot be explained merely as political maneuvering necessary to secure ratification.

Nor did the Federalists become persuaded that their objections to a bill of rights in the abstract were unfounded. They still believed that a bill of rights would be ineffective, even dangerous, if construed in an improper manner. Madison, announcing his change of mind in a letter to Thomas Jefferson, remarked, "My own opinion has always been in favor of a bill of rights, provided it be so framed as not to imply powers not meant to be included in the enumeration." In other words, if a bill of rights could be framed in a way that avoided the Federalists' objections, it might serve some useful purpose.

Madison's statement explains why he took the lead in writing the amendments that were considered by the First Congress. His intent was to frame the amendments in a way that would not undermine what had been achieved at the Convention. For one, Madison proposed to insert the amendments in the body of the Constitution, alongside other rights and protections already in the text, rather than placing them outside the Constitution as amendments to it. This would avoid a central problem that we encounter today, namely that the public's focus (and reverence) is drawn away from the Constitution and toward the amendments.

Second, having been rebuffed in that attempt by his colleagues in Congress, Madison was careful not to actually call the proposed amendments a bill of rights. Thus, the term "bill of rights" is not to be found in the preamble to the first 10 amendments to the Constitution. Strictly speaking, what we today call the Bill of Rights are 10 separate amendments, and they were to be considered as separate provisions rather than a single document. In a subtle but important move, the First Congress responded to the call for a bill of rights by providing a number of "declaratory and restrictive clauses" to be considered for ratification. This is also demonstrated by the fact that only 10 of the 12 proposed amendments were ratified in 1791. If the 12 amendments were to be considered as a single bill of rights, it would have been necessary to give an affirmative or negative vote to these amendments as a whole.

By framing the amendments in this way, Madison pointed back to the Declaration of Independence as the philosophic statement of rights and first principles; the amendments were not intended to replace or revise what had been set forth in that document. Therefore, the amendments should not be construed as enlarging the grant of power to the federal government by the Constitution, nor could they be thought to serve as a sufficient definition of all the rights and privileges of citizens.

These points illustrate the crucial importance of the Ninth and Tenth Amendments. Those amendments were drafted and ratified to prevent the Constitution from becoming a carte blanche of authority to an unlimited government. Neglect of these amendments by the public as well as the courts has been so conspicuous as to illustrate the force of the Federalists' original objections to a bill of rights. Yet for Madison, these amendments were central. They were intended to prevent the false interpretations that might be placed upon the provisions enumerating powers in the Constitution.

The Purpose of the Bill of Rights

There is one final question to be answered: Even if Madison believed that a bill of rights could be framed—as ours surely was—with the intent of preventing the implication of powers not granted to the government by the Constitution, what benefit could be gained by it? Was it not Madison who argued most forcefully that we cannot trust in parchment barriers? The answer is that

Madison indeed thought ambition would counteract ambition, to "oblige the government to control itself"—this was the idea of checks and balances. But it does not explain how the Founders proposed to safeguard individual liberty from tyranny of the majority, rather than tyranny of the rulers over the ruled. The safeguard of individual liberty, Madison reasoned, must lie with the people themselves. It is the people who must be responsible for defending their liberties. And a bill of rights, Madison and his colleagues finally concluded, might support public understanding and knowledge of individual liberty that would assist citizens in the task of defending their liberties.

A bill of rights, they saw, could serve the noble purpose of public education and edification. As Madison confided to Jefferson, "The political truths declared in that solemn manner acquire by degrees the character of fundamental maxims of free Government, and as they become incorporated with the national sentiment, counteract the impulses of interest and passion."

From this view, our first 10 amendments are still important today, in their text and substance, beyond their legal effect. They still call upon us to study them for the sake of knowing our liberties and defending them from all encroachments. Although these amendments may be nothing more than "parchment barriers," they can still provide a bulwark against encroachments on our rights. For as Hamilton wrote in Federalist 84, the security of liberty, "whatever fine declarations may be inserted in any constitution respecting it, must altogether depend on public opinion, and on the general spirit of the people and of the government. And here, after all…must we seek for the only solid basis of all our rights."

> "*The truth is that anyone interested in the political and legal issues of the day can and should look to the Ninth Amendment for guidance.*"

The Constitution Already Guarantees a Broad Range of "Human Rights"

Daniel Farber

In the following viewpoint, Daniel Farber discusses a right that most people aren't aware of—the Ninth Amendment, which is a protection of "unenumerated rights." Farber explains how it protects human rights that almost all people recognize, but that the government often does not protect. Farber's reading of the Ninth Amendment also settles a question about the concept of "originalism," which will come up later in this volume. Daniel Farber is an author and professor of law at the University of California at Berkeley.

As you read, consider the following questions:

1. Did the founders see the Constitution as giving citizens rights, or recognizing rights they naturally had?
2. How might more attention to the ninth amendment reshape how we think about the Constitution?
3. How do you think people on different sides of the political spectrum might respond to the ideas presented in this essay?

Everyone knows about the First Amendment right of free speech and the Fifth Amendment right to avoid self-incrimination. Even the once-forgotten Second Amendment, with its "right to bear arms," has reemerged in public debate. But few people know about the Ninth Amendment, which reaffirms in broad terms rights "retained by the people." Indeed, the Ninth flies so far under the radar that it has rarely been mentioned even by the Supreme Court.

What a pity. Even more, what a terrible oversight: the Ninth Amendment bears directly on such modern-day constitutional issues as abortion, the right to die, and gay rights.

The Ninth Amendment is key to understanding how the Founding Fathers thought about the liberties they expected Americans to enjoy under the Constitution. They did not believe that they were creating these liberties in the Bill of Rights. Instead, they were merely acknowledging some of the rights that no government could properly deny.

The history of the Constitution reveals the purpose of the Ninth and the Founders' intent: to protect what constitutional lawyers call unenumerated rights—those rights the Founder assumed and felt no need to specify in the Bill of Rights. Unenumerated rights include, for example, the right to privacy. In the America of today, unenumerated rights account for freedoms like a woman's right to abortion…

The truth is that anyone interested in the political and legal issues of the day can and should look to the Ninth Amendment for guidance.

The Ninth Amendment is paired with an almost equally forgotten provision, the Privileges or Immunities Clause (P or I Clause) of the Fourteenth Amendment, which draws from the same intellectual roots. The Ninth Amendment is like the rest of the original Bill of Rights: it speaks only to limits on federal power rather than to the powers of state governments. Limitations on state governments came along later, with the post-Civil War Fourteenth Amendment. Thus, the Ninth Amendment addresses the federal government; the Fourteenth addresses the states.

The human rights vision that survived the Civil War and was confirmed by the Fourteenth Amendment consciously complements that of the Founders. Confronting what these provisions really mean has the potential to reshape the way we think about the Constitution.

In particular, a look at this history helps us address the very controversial question of Supreme Court reliance on foreign law. The Framers thought that fundamental rights were embedded in what they called "the law of nations," and we should follow their lead in seeking inspiration abroad. However, their openness to foreign law is not universally shared today. When Justice Kennedy referred to foreign law in two judicial opinions on the issues of homosexuality and the death penalty, he was subject to an onslaught of criticism from legal commentators. Many of those same commentators question whether the United States is bound by international human rights laws, such as the Geneva Convention's prohibitions on mistreatment of prisoners …

The Ninth Amendment and the Debate over Fundamental Rights

Standing alone, the Ninth Amendment does not make any specific law unconstitutional. It is an explanation, not a command—like the FAQs found on many Web sites. In this case, the Frequently Asked Question is: "The Bill of Rights provides a list of specific rights that are protected from invasion by the federal government. Does this mean that the federal government can violate other rights if they aren't on the list?" The Ninth answers, "No. The Bill of Rights is not complete. Other rights exist, and the federal government must respect them." Indeed, as a supporter of the Constitution pointed out at the Pennsylvania ratification convention, "Our rights are not yet all known," so an enumeration was impossible. While it is true that history often fails to provide clear proof of what the Framers believed, there are exceptions. The Ninth Amendment is one of them.

How is all this playing out on our most vital constitutional front, the Supreme Court, today? The Court is sharply divided over whether the Constitution provides broad protection for human rights and just what those rights are. On one side have been those Justices who believe that the Constitution does give such broad protection—not just to those freedoms explicitly listed in the Bill of Rights but to other fundamental aspects of liberty. In honoring not merely the Framers' text but the intent behind it, these Justices have supported, for example, the right to abortion, the right of gays to have sexual relationships, and the right to die. More generally, these Justices have proclaimed: "At the heart of liberty is the right to define one's own concept of existence, of meaning, of the universe, and of the mystery of human life."

These Justices also honor the Framers' intent by looking beyond our national borders to seek the parameters of liberty. For example, in striking down a Texas law against homosexual conduct, the Court found it significant that the right to engage in homosexual relationships has "been accepted as an integral part of human freedom in many other countries." On today's bench, Justice Stevens has been a leading advocate of this view. However, its most influential voice is that of the more conservative Justice, Anthony Kennedy. Kennedy, a Reagan appointee, has become the *bête noire* of movement conservatives because he has so firmly defended basic rights and linked those rights to international law.

The opposing side is led by Justice Antonin Scalia, another Reagan appointee. As a former law professor at the University of Chicago and the University of Virginia, and now as a judge, Scalia has spent years working out an elaborate constitutional theory of originalism. He has consistently dissented from the entire line of human rights cases, arguing that abortion, gay rights, and end-of-life decisions should all be left entirely to the political process. This is a view that has powerful backing outside the Supreme Court. President Bush has renewed calls for strict construction of the Constitution (by which he means strict limits on individual rights, but apparently not strict construction of the powers of the presidency!).

More extremist views, replete with threats of impeachment or other unprecedented actions to rein in judges, can be found in Congress and among the Right's cultural leadership. Nothing is more anathema to these critics than the Court's reliance on foreign judicial precedents as a source of guidance in interpreting the Constitution. Justice Scalia warned of the Court's "dangerous" references to foreign law, adding that "this Court … should not impose foreign moods, fads, or fashions on Americans." He and his fellow critics see no connection between broader conceptions of human rights and constitutional law. They refuse to look seriously at what the Framers believed, how they saw the world.

Some conservatives also seemingly misunderstand the very idea of constitutional rights. Are basic rights like free speech or privacy created by the US Constitution? For many conservatives, these rights are merely the historical product of particular language adopted a century or two in the past; they have no broader roots or implications. If so, Justice Kennedy was surely wrong in the Texas sodomy case when he examined a much broader range of sources, including how states interpret their own constitutions, the actions taken by state legislatures to decriminalize sodomy, and the rulings of international tribunals. These sources are relevant only if we ask a broader question: "Are there good grounds for considering this to be a basic human right?" If that is the question, then actions by state legislatures, state judges, and international human rights tribunals are all persuasive authorities. The Founders certainly understood the law of nations and basic liberty in this way.

Rephrasing the question in these terms also rebuts another powerful argument against providing constitutional protection for human rights. Justice Scalia and others have argued that going beyond the specifics of the Bill of Rights would give the Supreme Court unlimited discretion to decide what parts of liberty are fundamental. This was the real concern that led Judge Bork to call the Ninth Amendment an inkblot: the fear that if we paid any attention to the Ninth Amendment at all, we would be mesmerized into giving the federal judiciary a blank check. This is much less problematic if the courts are guided by a broader community of opinion, including our own state decision makers as well as international authorities.

To see what is at stake, consider a 1927 Supreme Court case that upheld compulsory sterilization. The Virginia statute involved in the case established a procedure for sterilizing people with mental retardation who lived in state institutions, based on the idea that mental disability was inherited. The statute was challenged by a woman who was about to be sterilized. As later historical research revealed, she actually did not have a mental disability at all; she simply had been sent to an institution by her foster parents because she had become pregnant. In any event, the Supreme Court could not see any problem with the Virginia statute: "It is better for all the world, if instead of waiting to execute degenerate offspring for crime, or to let them starve for their imbecility, society can prevent those who are manifestly unfit from continuing their kind ... Three generations of imbeciles are enough." By 1935, over 20,000 forced sterilizations had been performed in the United States as a result of this decision.

If mainstream conservatives like Bork and Scalia are right, there is no constitutional barrier to these laws, because the Framers failed to predict this abuse and explicitly ban it. This is exactly the kind of reasoning that the Ninth Amendment was designed to guard against. A better understanding of the Ninth Amendment can do a great deal to clarify the current debate over fundamental rights, laying a firm foundation for the views of Justice Kennedy and other leading judges. Correspondingly, a true understanding of the Ninth Amendment is deadly to Justice Scalia's position.

Libertarians, who dislike government regulation of all kinds, agree with part of my argument, and I have found much of their historical research useful. They, too, would find the Amendment to be a source of real legal guidance. But they swing too far in the opposite direction from conservatives like Scalia. While Scalia wants the Ninth Amendment to protect nothing, the libertarians want it to protect virtually everything. They see in it the basis of a revolutionary return to the small government ideas of the early nineteenth century. But this is a gross overreading of the Amendment. It was meant to protect fundamental human rights, not just the right to do whatever you want whenever you want.

...[H]ere are some of the things I believe are among the unenumerated rights protected by the Constitution under the Ninth Amendment, backed up by the Fourteenth:

- The right to engage in private sexual acts between consenting adults. The Supreme Court was completely correct to strike down state sodomy laws.
- The right of reproductive autonomy, including the use of contraceptives and access to abortion as well as freedom from forced sterilization. Abortion is not an absolute right. The state can regulate to protect potential life, particularly later in pregnancy, so long as the burden placed on the pregnant woman is not too severe.
- The right to an adequate basic education. The Supreme Court has explicitly rejected this as a fundamental constitutional right, but many state courts have interpreted their state constitutions to protect this right. The Supreme Court would do well to follow their lead.
- The right to travel within the United States and to enter and leave the country freely (subject to clearly demonstrated national security needs).
- The right to government protection from private violence: when the government knows of the violence and has the resources to deal with the problem, it cannot simply sit on its hands. The Supreme Court has ruled that the state has every right to sit by while a Libertarians, who dislike government regulation of all kinds, small boy is beaten into a permanent coma by his father, even though the state knows all about what is going on. I would overturn that decision.

- The right to refuse unwanted medical treatment, including the right of terminally ill patients to reject life support.

But not everything is protected as a fundamental right. Here are some things that are not:

- The right of a terminally ill patient to prescribed medication with which to commit suicide.
- The right of businesses to be free from government regulation of their contracts with employees and customers.
- The right of individuals to use their property however they want, without regard to the public interest.

> *"To protect the Constitution from hasty alteration, the framers wrote Article V."*

The Constitution Can Be Amended Both Formally and Informally

Lumen Learning

The Bill of Rights, of course, is a set of amendments to the Constitution. The procedures for amending the Constitution are addressed in Article V. The authors of the following viewpoint explain what those procedures are, why they were included in the Constitution, and how they are put into play today. In addition, in the closing section on informal methods of amending the Constitution, this viewpoint brings up some concepts—societal change and judicial review—that you will read more about in later chapters.

As you read, consider the following questions:
1. What article of the Constitution addresses amending the Constitution?
2. What sized majority is required for Congress to pass amendments in both the House and Senate?
3. How do societal change and judicial review operate as de-facto amendments to the Constitution?

To protect the Constitution from hasty alteration, the framers of the Constitution wrote Article V.

Article V of the US Constitution

The Articles of Confederation made amending the law very difficult, as all states had to agree to an amendment before it could pass. A unanimous vote had the potential to completely stall crucial change. However, the Framers of the Constitution worried that too many changes would harm the democratic process. To protect the Constitution from hasty alteration, the framers wrote Article V. This article specified how to amend the Constitution, showing that the Constitution could adapt to changing conditions with an understanding that such changes required deliberation.

Proposing and Ratifying Amendments

There are two ways to propose amendments: First, states may call for a convention. This has never been used due to fears it would reopen the entire Constitution for revision. The other way is for Congress to pass amendments by a two-thirds majority in both the House and Senate.

There are two additional ways to approve an amendment: One is through ratification by three-fourths of state legislatures. Alternatively, an amendment can be ratified by three-fourths of specially convoked state convention. This process was used during the Prohibition era. Those in favor of ending Prohibition feared that the 21st Amendment (set to repeal the 18th Amendment prohibiting the sale and consumption of alcohol) would be blocked by conservative state legislatures. On December 5, 1933, these so-called "wets" asked for specially called state conventions and ratified repeal. Thus it was proved that a constitutional amendment can be stopped by one-third of either chamber of Congress or one-fourth of state legislatures.

Restrictions to the Amendment Process

The amendment process originally came with restrictions protecting some agreements that the Great Compromise had settled during the Constitutional Convention.

The Great Compromise (also called the Connecticut Compromise) was an agreement that large and small states reached during the Constitutional Convention of 1787. In part, the agreement defined the legislative structure and representation that each state would have under the US Constitution. It called for a bicameral legislature along with proportional representation in the lower house, but required the upper house to be weighted equally between the states. This agreement led to the Three-Fifths Compromise, which meant less populous Southern states were allowed to count three-fifths of all non-free people toward population counts and allocations.

Thus, Article V of the US Constitution, ratified in 1788, prohibited any constitutional amendments before 1808 which would affect the foreign slave trade, the tax on slave trade, or the direct taxation on provisions of the constitution. Also, no amendment may affect the equal representation of states in the Senate without a state's consent.

Formal Methods of Amending the Constitution

The formal amendment processes are enumerated in Article V of the Constitution.

Formal Processes

The formal processes of amending the constitution are the processes articulated in Article V of the Constitution. These are the Congressional method and the Constitutional Convention methods.

In theory the two houses first adopt a resolution indicating that they deem an amendment necessary. This procedure, however, has never actually been used. The US Senate and the US House of Representatives instead directly proceed to the adoption of a joint resolution; thus, they mutually propose the amendment with the implication that both bodies "deem" the amendment to be "necessary." All amendments presented so far have been proposed and implemented as codicils, appended to the main body of the Constitution.

If at least two-thirds of the legislatures of the states make the request, Congress is then required to call a convention for the purpose of proposing amendments. This provision, many scholars argue, allows for a check on the power of the Congress to limit potential constitutional amendments. The state legislatures have, in times past, used their power to apply for a national convention in order to pressure Congress into proposing a desired amendment.

A classic example of this was demonstrated starting in the late 1890s. During that period a movement to amend the Constitution to provide for the direct election of US Senators caused such proposals to regularly pass the House of Representatives only to die in the Senate. As time went by, more and more state legislatures adopted resolutions demanding that a convention be called. In response to this pressure the Senate finally relented and approved what later became the Seventeenth Amendment for fear that such a convention—if permitted to assemble—might stray to include issues above and beyond the direct election of US Senators.

The President has no formal role in the constitutional amendment process. Article One provides that "every order, resolution, or vote, to which the concurrence of the Senate and House of Representatives may be necessary (except on a question of adjournment) shall be presented to the President of the United States; and before the same shall take effect, shall be approved by him, or being disapproved by him, shall be repassed by two thirds of the Senate and House of Representatives."

As previously stated, the Constitution requires that at least two-thirds of the members present of both the House of Representatives and the Senate the agree to a joint resolution which proposes a constitutional amendment. However, in *Hollingsworth* v. *Virginia* (1798), the Supreme Court held that it is not necessary to place constitutional amendments before the President for signature and that, by the same logic, the President is powerless to veto a proposed constitutional amendment.

Ratification

After being officially proposed, a constitutional amendment must then be ratified either by the legislatures of at least three-fourths of the states, or by conventions in the same proportion of states. Of the 27 amendments to the Constitution that have been ratified, Congress has specified the method of ratification through state conventions for only one: the 21st Amendment, which became part of the Constitution in 1933.

Most states hold elections specifically for the purpose of choosing delegates to such conventions. New Mexico state law provides that the members of its legislature be the delegates at such a state ratification convention. It is unclear whether this New Mexico state law violates the United States Constitution.

Although a proposed amendment is effective after three-fourths of the states ratify it, states have, in many instances, ratified an amendment that has already become law, often for symbolic reasons. The states unanimously ratified the Bill of Rights; the Thirteenth Amendment, abolishing slavery; the Fourteenth Amendment, providing for equal protection and due process; the Fifteenth Amendment, prohibiting racial discrimination in voting; and the Nineteenth Amendment, granting women a federal constitutional right to vote. In several cases, the ratification process took over a century.

Informal Methods of Amending the Constitution: Societal Change and Judicial Review

The formal amendment process is one of two major ways to amend the constitution.

The United States Constitution can be changed informally. Informal amendments mean that the Constitution does not specifically list these processes as forms of amending the Constitution, but because of change in society or judicial review changed the rule of law de facto. These methods depend on interpretations of what the constitution says and on interpretive understanding of the underlying intent. This type of change occurs in two major forms: through circumstantial change and through judicial review.

Societal Change

Sometimes society changes, leading to shifts in how constitutional rights are applied. For example, originally only land-holding white males could vote in federal elections. Due to a burgeoning middle class at the peak of the Industrial Revolution in the 1800s, society became focused on expanding rights for the middle and working classes. This led to the right to vote being extended to more and more people. However, formal recognition of the right of poor whites and black males, and later of women, was only fully secured in the Fifteenth Amendment (1870) and the Nineteenth Amendment (1920).

Judicial Review

In the United States, federal and state courts at all levels, both appellate and trial, are able to review and declare the constitutionality of legislation relevant to any case properly within their jurisdiction. This means that they evaluate whether a law is or is not in agreement with the Constitution and its intent. In American legal language, "judicial review" refers primarily to the adjudication of constitutionality of statutes, especially by the Supreme Court of the United States. This is commonly held to have been established by Chief Justice John Marshall in the case of *Marbury* v. *Madison*, which was argued before the Supreme Court in 1803. A number of other countries whose constitutions provide for such a review of constitutional compatibility of primary legislation have established special constitutional courts with authority to deal with this issue. In these systems, no other courts are competent to question the constitutionality of primary legislation.

The Twenty-Seven Amendments of the US Constitution

The twenty-seven amendments serve two purposes: to protect the liberties of the people and to change original codes from the constitution.

There are 27 amendments to the constitution, the first 10 being the Bill of Rights. The Bill of Rights is the collective name for the first ten amendments to the United States Constitution. These limitations serve to protect the natural rights of liberty and property. They guarantee a number of personal freedoms, limit the government's power in judicial and other proceedings, and reserve some powers to the states and the public. While originally the amendments applied only to the federal government, most of their provisions have since been held to apply to the states by way of the Fourteenth Amendment.

The other amendments have been added over time, mostly via the processes mentioned in Article V of the Constitution. The 11th secures the right to sue a state. The 12th defines the election of President and Vice President and the fallback system if one should die in office. The 13th abolishes slavery. The 14th specifies the post-Civil War requirements and notes that freed slaves are citizens. The 15th specifically dictates that all races have full rights. The 16th modifies the tax system. The 17th lays out the system for replacement of senators. The 18th banned alcohol. The 19th gives women the right to vote. The 20th patches some basic government functions. The 21st makes the 18th amendment inactive, thereby un-banning alcohol. The 22nd amendment states that no one can be elected President more than 2 terms. The 23rd modifies the Electoral College. The 24th states that no one can be kept from voting because of tax status. The 25th reinforces the replacement system for the President and Vice President. The 26th moves the voting age to 18. The 27th deals with the payment of representatives.

Periodical and Internet Sources Bibliography

The following articles have been selected to supplement the diverse views presented in this chapter.

David Azerrad, "How James Madison Saved the Constitution by Writing the Bill of Rights," *Federalist*, December 28, 2016. http://thefederalist.com/2016/12/28/james-madison-saved-constitution-month-writing-bill-rights/.

Charles C. W. Cooke, "Why the Bill of Rights Would Never Pass Today," *National Review,* May 4, 2015. http://www.nationalreview.com/article/417828/why-bill-rights-would-never-pass-today-charles-c-w-cooke.

Garrett Epps, "What Does the Constitution Actually Say about Voting Rights?: or: How the *Shelby* Ruling is Like Starving a Sog to Death," *Atlantic*, August 19, 2013. https://www.theatlantic.com/national/archive/2013/08/what-does-the-constitution-actually-say-about-voting-rights/278782/.

Jill Lepore, "The Rule of History: Magna Carta, the Bill of Rights, and the Hold of Time," *New Yorker,* April 20, 2015. https://www.newyorker.com/magazine/2015/04/20/the-rule-of-history.

David John Morotta. "The Ninth Amendment: The Value of Our Unenumerated Rights," *Forbes*, December 16, 2012. https://www.forbes.com/sites/davidmarotta/2012/12/16/the-ninth-amendment-the-value-of-our-unenumerated-rights/#1b9565c8f604.

New York Times, editorial board, "When the Bill of Rights Had 12 Amendments, *New York Times*, July 2, 2013. http://www.nytimes.com/2013/07/03/opinion/when-the-bill-of-rights-had-12-amendments.html?mtrref=www.google.com&gwh=BC1D0EC082BB0CDBD003C75E36B08B2F&gwt=pay&assetType=opinion.

Devin Watkins, "Unenumerated Rights Are Not Second-Class, Rights," *National Review*, February 9, 2017. http://www.nationalreview.com/article/444759/ninth-amendment-rights-protection.

OPPOSING
VIEWPOINTS®
SERIES

CHAPTER 2

How Should We Interpret the Bill of Rights?

Chapter Preface

In 1803, the Supreme Court decided, in *Marbury* v. *Madison,* that courts had the power to invalidate a law, if the court deemed that the law was in conflict with the Constitution. This case established the principle of judicial review. How those decisions are best made, however, is still a matter of no small amount of controversy.

This chapter opens with a slightly closer look at the debates of the Constitution, including those surrounding the inclusion of the Bill of Rights. This discussion sets up the following viewpoints, which outline and examine in some detail the basic philosophies of judicial interpretation and judicial review. On the one side are those who firmly believe that when interpreting laws and enforcing the protections contained in the Bill of Rights (and other matters in the Constitution), the courts should base their judgments on and only on the meanings of the words in the Constitution, the intentions of the founders, or some combination of both. This view is usually called "originalism."

Others argue that the Constitution should be a "living document," that is, its meaning should change as our society evolves and changes. Law that made sense in 1787 would not necessarily apply now. Just one example: if the Constitution were interpreted with absolute historical accuracy (based on the beliefs and intent of the founders), women, African Americans, and anyone who did not own property would be prohibited from voting or serving in public office. Opponents to the living document approach point out that if we continue to re-interpret the Constitution as we go, the document will quickly cease to have any meaning at all. In practice, all sides tend to deal with the issue with some combination of approaches. However, that is not always what they say when making their cases.

Many of the following viewpoints contain references to US Supreme Court Justice Antonin Scalia. Scalia, who died in 2016, was one of the most vocal proponents of originalist interpretations of the Constitution.

> *"Generally speaking, there are two main ways in which court justices, judges, and legal analysts interpret laws and constitutions: As living documents that evolve as the culture changes, and as fixed documents whose meaning never changes from the time that they were written until now."*

Judicial Interpretation Is Similar to Interpretation of Religious Texts

Bruce A. Robinson

In the following viewpoint, Bruce A. Robinson discusses the different philosophies that are often used to interpret the Bill of Rights. The author compares approaches to the interpretation of the Constitution to approaches to the interpretation of religious texts. As Robinson points out, there is an unquestionable difference between interpreting the Constitution based on modern standards and values, and interpreting it as it might have been interpreted at the time of its writing. Robinson is coordinator and lead author of the website Religious Tolerance.

"Judicial Philosophies: How Judges Interpret Constitutions and Laws," by B.A. Robinson, Ontario Consultants on Religious Tolerance, July 17, 2017, at http://www.religioustolerance.org/scotuscon6.htm. Reprinted by permission.

As you read, consider the following questions:

1. How has the definition of "cruel and unusual punishment" changed over time?
2. What are the subtle differences between "originalism," "textualism," and "literalism"?
3. How does textualism overcome some of the obvious problems of originalism according to this article?

People can generally agree on what the text of a Constitution or law says; they often have problems over interpretation. This is when they cannot reach a consensus on what it means in today's culture.

Generally speaking, there are two main ways in which court justices, judges, and legal analysts interpret laws and constitutions:

- As living documents that evolve as the culture changes, and
- As fixed documents whose meaning never changes from the time that they were written until now.

There is a correspondence concerning between the religion and law in the interpretation of text:

- Liberal and progressive wings of religions tend to interpret holy books as living documents, by considering the present-day culture, evolving concepts of morality, one's personal experience and the findings of science. Thus, liberal and progressive Christians reject many passages in the Bible that they consider to be immoral by today's standards.
- Fundamentalists, other evangelicals and some mainline Christians generally interpret biblical passages literally as the "Word of God," and act accordingly, unless a different interpretation is obviously needed.

Interpreting Laws and Constitutions as Living Documents

The document's meaning is viewed as continually evolving to meet the culture's changing beliefs, practices, and knowledge. This has been the position of most of the justices of the US Supreme Court in recent decades. It is also the viewpoint used by the Supreme Court of Canada and similar high courts of many other western countries.

Justice Scalia [did] not share this philosophy. He attacked what he called a "conventional fallacy" in which the meaning of the constitution is interpreted: "…from age to age [as] whatever the society (or perhaps the Court) thinks it ought to mean."[1]

A *Focus on the Family* news report in 2006-FEB said that Justice Scalia:

> …sharply criticized those who say the US Constitution should be interpreted as a "living document"—one that should change with the times. According to the Associated Press, Scalia told a gathering of the Federalist Society … "you would have to be an idiot to believe that. The Constitution is not a living organism, it is a legal document," he said. "It says something and doesn't say other things."

One example of the living document philosophy is found In the US Supreme Court's ruling in *Trop* v. *Dulles* (1958).[2] The court discussed the evolution over time of the meaning of the "cruel and unusual punishment" clause in the US Constitution's Eighth Amendment. The Court had earlier recognized that: "… the words of the Amendment are not precise…and that their…scope is not static. They stated in *Trop* v. *Dulles* that "The Amendment must draw its meaning from the evolving standards of decency that mark the progress of a maturing society."

In recent years, some justices of the US Supreme Court have gone outside American society and have incorporated references to cultural developments in other Western countries in their rulings.[3] In 2002, the US Supreme Court ruled in *Atkins* v. *Virginia* that the execution of mentally retarded murderers is cruel and unusual punishment and is thus unconstitutional under the Eight Amendment to the US Constitution.

Amnesty International commented:

> The Atkins ruling overturned a 1989 decision, *Penry* v. *Lynaugh*, by finding that "standards of decency" in the USA had evolved in the intervening years to the point at which a "national consensus" had emerged against such executions—primarily reflected in state-level legislation banning the execution of the mentally retarded. From an international human rights perspective, an encouraging footnote attached to the Atkins opinion acknowledged that "within the world community, the imposition of the death penalty for crimes committed by mentally retarded offenders is overwhelmingly disapproved."[4]

Religious and social conservatives frequently use phrases such as "judicial activists" or as "judges legislating from the bench" to refer to judges and justices who:

- Interpret laws and the constitution as living documents, or
- Detect a conflict between a piece of legislation and the constitution, and rule consider the constitution supreme.

However, conservatives generally complain only when that interpretation conflicts with their position.

Interpret Laws and Constitutions as Enduring Documents

This theory of interpretation is often called "strict constructionism." It interprets a legal document as meaning "today not what current society (much less the Court) thinks it ought to mean, but what it meant when it was adopted."[5] It requires a judge to apply a law or constitution only as it was written.

The term has a second meaning. It is often loosely used as an umbrella term that covers three slightly different philosophies:

Originalism

The belief that the meaning of the US Constitution is static, fixed, and knowable. It is to be interpreted today in the way in which the authors originally intended it. One might look at the writings of the framers of the constitution for guidance. This is a very popular theory among political conservatives.

A weakness of this theory is that the framers held diverse opinions at the time. Also, the Constitution was ratified by delegates at 13 state conventions who themselves held diverse beliefs. Whose opinions should rule? Finally, as US Constitution Online states—with a possible reference to Thomas Jefferson:

> "... do the opinions of a small, homogeneous group from 200 years ago have the respect of the huge, diverse population of today? To a black woman, how much trust can be placed in the thoughts of a white slave owner who's been dead for generations?"[6]

US Supreme Court Justices Antonin Scalia and Clarence Thomas are often referred to as originalists in matters of Constitutional interpretation.[7]

Textualism

This is the belief that the Constitution's or law's ordinary meaning as perceived by reasonable persons living at the time that it was adopted should govern its interpretation today. Other factors are considered irrelevant, including:

- The actual intention of the body that created and passed the document.
- The exact problem that it was intended to solve at the time it was written.
- Whether the law is just.
- Whether the law can be justified, etc.[8,9]

Justice Scalia is generally regarded as a textualist in the interpretation of legislation.

Literalism

The belief that a constitution or law should be interpreted according to the literal meaning of its words at the time the document was authorized. Thus:

> … the contemporary writings of the Framers are not relevant to any interpretation of the Constitution. The only thing one needs to interpret the Constitution is a literal reading of the words contained therein, with an expert knowledge in the 18th century meaning of those words.
>
> The debates leading to the final draft are not relevant, the *Federalist Papers* are not relevant—only the words. The historical literalist takes a similar look at the Constitution as an originalist does, but the literalist has no interest in expanding beyond the text for answers to questions.[10]

To further confuse the situation, the term "strict constructionism" has a third meaning: it is often used very loosely to refer to any judge, justice or legal analyst who is very conservative. It is often difficult to determine the term's precise meaning in a give text.

Notes

1. "Religion, Politics and the Death Penalty," Pew Forum on Religion & Public Life, 2002-JAN, at: http://www.pewtrusts.com/

2. "Trop v. Dulles, 356 U.S. 86 (1958)." text is at: http://supreme.justia.com/

3. "Trop v. Dulles," U.S. Supreme Court, 1958-MAR-31, at: http://caselaw.lp.findlaw.com/

4. "The execution of mentally ill offenders," Amnesty International, at: http://web.amnesty.org/

5. Antonin Scalaia, "God's Justice and Ours," First Things 123, 2002-MAY, Page 17 to 21.

6. "Constitutional Interpretation," U./S. Constitution Online, at: http://www.usconstitution.net/

7. "Originalism," Wikipedia, at: http://en.wikipedia.org/

8. Antonin Scalia, "A Matter of Interpretation: Federal Courts and the Law," edited by Amy Gutmann, Princeton University Press, (1997), Page 13. Cited in: Ralph A. Rossum, "The Textualist Jurisprudence of Justice Scalia," Claremont McKenna College, 2009, at: http://www.claremontmckenna.edu/

9. "Textualism," Wikipedia at: http://en.wikipedia.org/wiki/Textualism

10. "Constitutional Interpretation," Essays.cc at: http://www.essays.cc/

> "*[The founders] spoke in general terms because they expected that people who came along later would have to do their part.*"

Focus on the Constitution Rather Than on the Supreme Court

Ari Shapiro

In the following viewpoint, Ari Shapiro discusses liberals' attempts to frame their position in the ongoing debate of how the Bill of Rights should be interpreted. This piece was written in 2009, when Barack Obama was president. Obama was an expert in Constitutional law, and the justices he placed on the court were not originalists, textualists, or literalists. Ari Shapiro is host of the National Public Radio news program All Things Considered.

As you read, consider the following questions:

1. Which former Supreme Court justice was the prime defender of an original interpretation of the Constitution?
2. What word did President Obama use to describe what he was looking for in a potential justice?
3. Why did one law professor compare the Supreme Court to a husband in a French farce?

A few years ago, the online magazine *Slate* hosted a contest. Senior Editor Dahlia Lithwick asked readers—If you don't believe in interpreting the Constitution the way it was written more than 200 years ago, what do you believe in?

"The left was in this funny defensive crouch," says Lithwick. "It was saying, 'Whatever we're for, we know we're not for [Supreme Court Justice Antonin] Scalia and originalism.'"

Scalia is the *bete noir* of the liberal legal establishment and the prime spokesman for the view that the meaning of the Constitution does not change over time. He defended his position in a 2008 NPR interview, saying, "If you somehow adopt a philosophy that the Constitution itself is not static, but rather it morphs from age to age to say whatever it ought to say—which is probably whatever the people would want it to say—you eliminate the whole purpose of a Constitution. And that is essentially what the so-called living Constitution leaves you with."

On Slate.com, Lithwick asked for a liberal counterargument, and the mail poured in. "I think the conclusion was originalism just has a better agent," says Lithwick. "They have better PR, and living constitutionalism has really lost the PR war and needs better representation."

That was four years ago. Now, liberals are back in the fray.

A Unique Time to Present a Countertheory

They see this as a unique moment in American history: the first time in decades that progressives could actually win the legal debate over theories of constitutional interpretation.

For the first time in 15 years, the country is evaluating a Supreme Court nominee who does not believe in originalism. The president is a Democrat who used to teach constitutional law. And progressive legal scholars have published a pile of books exploring the best alternative to conservative legal theories.

"In the public debate, it has been a great challenge for the liberal and progressive side to capture this notion in a bumper sticker," says Goodwin Liu, editor of the new book *Keeping Faith with the Constitution.* Liu teaches law at the University of California, Berkeley, and he chairs the board of the American Constitution Society, a progressive legal group.

Philosophies in the Running

"Living constitutionalism" is just one of the many phrases fighting to be the progressive constitutional standard-bearer. Other contenders include "democratic constitutionalism," "redemptive constitutionalism," "constitutional fidelity" and "progressive originalism."

As Liu points out, President Obama recently added another word to the mix.

"We have felled many trees coming up with a term," says Liu, "and then President Obama mentions a single word—empathy—and the entire debate swirls around that word."

In a news conference after Supreme Court Justice David Souter announced his retirement, Obama said, "I view that quality of empathy, of understanding and identifying with people's hopes and struggles, as an essential ingredient for arriving at just decisions and outcomes."

Obama has long advocated a view that the Constitution must be interpreted to reflect the changing norms and understandings of an evolving society. In his book *The Audacity of Hope*, he wrote, "Before the ink on the constitutional parchment was dry, arguments had erupted, not just about minor provisions, but about first principles. Not just between peripheral figures, but within the revolution's very core."

A Living Tradition

Yale law professor Reva Siegel is one of the progressive legal scholars at the forefront of this debate. She argues that judges can neither ignore the past nor give it unquestioning loyalty.

"The Constitution is neither an agreement that was made by persons long dead, nor is it something that simply reflects the understandings of living Americans," Siegel says. "In fact, it's a living tradition that links the struggles, commitments and beliefs of Americans past, present and future."

Siegel co-edited the new book *The Constitution in 2020* with Yale law professor Jack Balkin.

Balkin argues that the Founding Fathers intentionally made some passages of the Constitution very specific—such as the requirement that the president be at least 35 years old—and other passages intentionally vague.

"They spoke in general terms because they expected that people who came along later would have to do their part," Balkin says. "They would have an obligation to continue the project."

Balkin describes that project of ongoing interpretation as true constitutional fidelity.

"Gobbledygook"

"I think that's gobbledygook," says Eric Posner, University of Chicago law professor. "It's just kind of a pun on what fidelity means."

Posner says he believes neither in originalism nor in the academic philosophies that liberals are describing.

"They have to come up with a better idea," Posner says. "And instead of coming up with a better idea, I think they're trying to figure out what the PR angle of originalism is and how to duplicate it."

Posner says he believes everyone is trying to disguise the fact that judges are basically political actors, on the left and right.

Even if these progressive ideas take hold, the courts will not shift any time soon. The Supreme Court has five solid conservative votes, and one new nominee won't change that.

Balkin is not worried.

"My view of the Supreme Court is sort of like the husband in the French farce," Balkin says. "He's always the last to know."

Balkin adds, "Essentially, stop bothering about the Supreme Court. Start thinking about what the Constitution means in the general public. The courts will catch up in good time."

> "*The executive and judicial branches have expanded their powers beyond the Founders' expectations over time.*"

The Balance of Power Intended by the Framers Has Tipped

Bill of Rights Institute

In the following viewpoint, authors from the Bill of Rights Institute begin by tracing the history of the concept of three roles of government and the development of the idea, so integral to the US system of government, of assigning those roles to separate governmental branches. They use quotes from the philosophers who inspired the founders, as well as the founders themselves, and describe how Madison interpreted and refined the concept by introducing a system of checks and balances. The Bill of Rights Institute offers education and development on American history and government for youth and teachers.

As you read, consider the following questions:

1. Why did the framers fear the accumulation of power in one branch of government?
2. What is at the heart of the Madisonian Model?
3. Why have the executive and judicial branches gained more power over the years?

The Founding Fathers were well-acquainted with a long-held tenet of government: the accumulation of power by a single person or body of government is the greatest threat to liberty. In fact, a celebrated feature of the Constitution, the separation of powers doctrine, developed over the course of many centuries.

As early as 350 B.C., Greek philosopher Aristotle observed in the Politics that every government, no matter its form, performed three distinct functions: "the deliberative, the magisterial, and the judicative." In modern terminology these activities correlate, respectively, to the legislative (law-making), executive (law-enforcing) and judicial (law interpretation) functions of government. While Aristotle identified these basic powers common to all governments, he did not necessarily suggest that they should be exercised by entirely different branches.

The principle that major governmental functions should be divided into different branches would be advanced centuries later. The French philosopher Baron de Montesquieu, "[t]he oracle… the celebrated Montesquieu," as James Madison referred to him, advocated three distinct and separate branches in which the general powers of government should be lodged. While John Locke made the case for separating the legislative and executive powers, Montesquieu provided the Founders with a convincing defense for an independent judiciary:

> When the legislative and executive powers are united in the same person, or in the same body of magistrates, there can be no liberty… Again, there is no liberty, if the judiciary power be not separated from the legislative and executive. Were it joined with the legislative, the life and liberty of the subject would be exposed to arbitrary control; for the judge would then be the legislator. Were it joined to the executive power, the judge might behave with violence and oppression. There would be an end to everything, were the same man, or the same body, whether of the nobles or of the people, to exercise those three powers, that of enacting laws, that of executing the public resolutions, and of trying the causes of individuals (Baron de Montesquieu, Spirit of Laws, 1748).

It was Montesquieu's vision of a truly separated, tripartite system that the Founding Fathers would come to adopt at the Constitutional Convention. Article I, Section 1 of the US Constitution vests legislative powers in a Congress of the United States, itself separated into a House of Representatives and a Senate. Article II, Section 1 vests executive authority in a President of the United States. Article III, Section 1 vests judicial authority in a single Supreme Court of the United States and "in such inferior Courts as the Congress may from time to time ordain and establish."

During the ratification debates from 1787 to 1788, some critics charged that upon close inspection the separation of powers in Articles I-III of the Constitution were not as complete as Montesquieu appeared to advocate and would tend toward an accumulation of power in one branch or another over time. The president, for example, has the power to accept or reject a bill duly passed by Congress, a seemingly legislative power. For its part, the Senate may approve or reject a presidential appointment to his own branch, a seemingly executive power.

The Constitution's critics were right; the Framers did not propose a "pure" separation of powers. Madison retorted that a "pure" separation of powers was neither what Montesquieu intended nor practical:

> [Montesquieu] did not mean that these [branches] ought to have no partial agency in, or no control over, the acts of each other. His meaning…can amount to no more than this, that where the whole power of one [branch] is exercised by the hands that hold the whole power of another, the fundamental principles of a free constitution are subverted. [T]here is not a single instance in which the several [branches] of power have been kept absolutely separate and distinct (James Madison, Federalist No. 47, 1788).

Implicit in Madison's argument was an interesting challenge to the very doctrine of separation of powers: what will prevent the accumulation of power in the absence of pure separation? The answer was to be found in a unique feature of the Constitution: the pairing of separated powers with an intricate system of checks

ORIGINALISM DOESN'T MAKE SENSE

Originalism does not reflect what the Supreme Court ever has done in interpreting the Constitution. The Court always has looked at the text and the underlying purpose and the original intent and traditions and precedents and contemporary social needs. Even the justices who most advocate originalism abandon it when it does not serve their purposes. Justices Scalia and Thomas, for example, are adamantly opposed to affirmative action and simply choose to ignore that the original intent of the equal protection clause was to allow race-conscious programs to benefit minorities. The Congress that ratified the Fourteenth Amendment, however, adopted many such efforts.

There is an obvious reason why originalism never has—and hopefully never will—be followed by a majority of the Court: it makes no sense to be governed in the 21st century by the intent of those in 1787 (or 1791 when the Bill of Rights was adopted or 1868 when the Fourteenth Amendment was ratified). Simple examples illustrate this. The Constitution uses the pronoun "he" to refer to the President and Vice President and the original understanding is that they would be men. An originalist would have to say that it is unconstitutional to elect a woman to these offices until the Constitution is amended.

"The Misguided Debate Over Constitutional Interpretation," by Erwin Chemerinsky, American Constitution Society, September 16, 2013.

and balances designed to give each branch fortifications against encroachments by the others. The "Madisonian Model," as it is now generally called, gave genuine and practical life to both the observation of Aristotle and the vision of Montesquieu.

At the heart of the Madisonian Model is ambition. A desire for power, influence, and authority is embedded deeply in human nature. For many people, the very word "ambition" smacks of greed, corruption, or a win-at-all-cost mentality.

Madison saw it differently. Ambition, if properly harnessed by good judgment and rooted in an appreciation for the benefits of constitutional republicanism, could work to advance the public good. It could be beneficial not only to the effective separation of powers but to limited government and liberty itself. In Federalist No. 51, James Madison stated:

> The great security against a gradual concentration of the several powers in the same [branch], consists in giving to those who administer each [branch], the necessary constitutional means, and personal motives, to resist encroachments of the others... Ambition must be made to counteract ambition. The interest of the man must be connected with the constitutional rights of the place (James Madison, Federalist No. 51, 1788).

In our system of separated powers, each branch of government is not only given a finite amount of power and authority but arrives at it through entirely different modes of election. Madison theorized that as it is the Constitution that grants each branch its power, honorable ambition that ultimately serves the highest interests of the people could work to maintain the separation. In other words, since Congress is not dependent on the presidency or the courts for either its authority or its election to office, members will jealously guard its power from encroachments by the other two branches and vice versa. For Madison, this organization of powers answered the great challenge of framing a limited government of separated powers: "first enabl[ing] the government to control the governed...and in the next place, oblig[ing] it to control itself" (James Madison, Federalist No. 51, 1788).

What does Madison's theory look like in practice? While it is the legislative branch that makes law, the president may check Congress by vetoing bills Congress has passed, preventing them from being enacted. In turn, Congress may enact a law over the president's objection by overriding his veto with a vote of two-thirds of both the House and Senate. The Supreme Court can then check both branches by declaring a law unconstitutional (known as judicial review), but the Supreme Court itself is checked by virtue of the fact the president and Senate appoint and approve, respectively, members of the Court. Furthermore, both the president and federal judges are subject to impeachment by Congress for "treason, bribery, or other high crimes and misdemeanors" (United States Constitution: Article II, Section 4).

By and large, Madison's model remains constitutionally intact, but many people wonder if our system still balances power, in reality and in practice, to the extent that he envisioned. Our checks and balances system reflects an understanding about republican government, held by many Founders, that the legislative branch should be the superior branch and, therefore, most in need of restraint. They reasoned that this is the case because "We the People" govern ourselves through the laws we give ourselves through our elected representatives in the legislative branch.

> The legislative [branch] derives superiority... [i]ts constitutional powers [are] more extensive, and less susceptible to precise limits... [it] is not possible to give each [branch] an equal [number of checks on the other branches] (James Madison, Federalist No. 48, 1788).

Some observers maintain that this conception of the legislative as the predominant branch is obsolete in modern times. The executive and judicial branches have expanded their powers beyond the Founders' expectations over time (i.e. executive orders, the role of the Supreme Court as the arbiter of laws at every level, not just the federal level.) Is Madison's assumption of legislative superiority true today? If you were asked to pick a branch to describe as "most powerful" would your answer mirror Madison's?

Despite disagreement as to how well it has worked, one characteristic of the checks and balances system cannot be denied: it encourages constant tension and conflict between the branches. That conflict, however, is frequently beneficial, and our Constitution smiles upon it.

> *"Any jurist who unswervingly sided with the law and steadfastly sidelined personal preferences would not be a human but an angel or automaton. Our benches lack both angels and automatons."*

Originalism Is a Complex Position

Saikrishna Bangalore Prakash

In the following viewpoint, Saikrishna Bangalore Prakash offers a defense of Justice Antonin Scalia, providing a great deal of insight into the judicial philosophies behind Scalia's decisions. Scalia's opinions were often controversial, but as the author suggests, they may have been far more nuanced than many of his detractors suggest. Saikrishna Bangalore Prakash is professor of law at the University of Virginia.

As you read, consider the following questions:

1. To which law professor is the viewpoint author responding in this piece?
2. What were Scalia's two "black beasts" according to the author?
3. What does the author say about claims that Scalia was bigoted?

"A Fool for the Original Constitution," *Harvard Law Review*, November 10, 2016. Reprinted by permission.

I confess that Justice Antonin Scalia was one of my heroes. He did not seem a demigod; he was no Washington, Lincoln, or Gandhi. Justice Scalia could be too pugnacious. He could vent against colleagues in ways that seemed counterproductive. But his wit, intellect, brio, and prose—well, these were marvels to behold.

For a spell, Professor Jamal Greene was of a similar mind. In a *New York Times* op-ed written shortly after Justice Scalia's passing, Greene said that "Antonin Scalia was my hero," that he had "looked up to [the Justice] for years," and that the Justice wielded "enormous influence." The praise reflected rather well on Greene. Unlike some, he perceived the virtues in an intellectual opponent. It took pluck for a liberal to confess, in public, his admiration for Justice Scalia. I suspect that some thought the op-ed was akin to a tribute to Orval Faubus.

Something happened over the spring or summer of 2016, from the pages of the *New York Times* to the pages of the *Harvard Law Review*. Greene's overflowing praise has dried up. Filling the void is a denial of Justice Scalia's influence and the claim that "[w]hether or not Justice Scalia was a bigot, his client—the law of chronic resistance to novelty—most certainly was." Greene sheepishly implies he gave in to some temptation when he wrote for the *Times*. I do not know what intervention or epiphany triggered this seismic shift, but the reversal, executed over a few months, is extraordinary.

My remarks largely track Greene's. I discuss Justice Scalia's guiding lights, elements underscored in his many writings and speeches. I briefly comment on what I consider minor blemishes in his jurisprudence. I discuss his outsized influence and why it likely will endure. Finally I make a few observations about Greene's claims that originalism is "regressive" and that Justice Scalia's critics had reason to carp that the Justice's jurisprudence and remarks were bigoted. To get down to brass tacks, Greene's latest pronouncements are off target. In contrast, his observations in the *Times* were spot on. Sometimes we are right the first time.

I. Influences

Where Greene discovers a two-part agenda, I perceive four influences that shaped Justice Scalia's jurisprudence. In addition to the two strands that Greene identifies—originalism and a preference for rules over—I perceive deep commitments to judicial restraint and tradition. As Greene correctly highlights, Justice Scalia is well known for his full-throated defenses of originalism. In part, this association stems from his highly influential and delightful essay, Originalism: The Lesser Evil. Justice Scalia also favored rules over standards, a partiality defended in The Rule of Law as a Law of Rules. The Justice believed that rules constrain the courts and supply predictability, whereas standards leave deep uncertainty about how judges will apply them.

Though Greene ably identifies these features of Justice Scalia's jurisprudence, I believe that he omits two more. First, Justice Scalia sought to restrain the courts. The preference for discerning rules in the law served that interest, for Justice Scalia believed that rules inhibit judicial lawmaking. But the preference for rules was but one factor behind the Justice's interest in judicial restraint. In advocating such restraint, the Justice channeled the counterreaction to the excesses of the Warren and Burger Courts. Justices on those Courts tended to see little difference between their preferences and the law, an inclination that predictably led those Justices to impose their preferences as law. Justice Scalia's insistence on rigorous adherence to exacting standing doctrines also reflected his desire to constrain the federal courts. The Justice was quick to criticize the predilection of the Supreme Court to act as a "nine-headed Caesar, giving thumbs-up or thumbs-down to whatever outcome, case by case, suits or offends its collective fancy."

The final strand emphasized tradition. "[W]hen a practice not expressly prohibited by the text of the Bill of Rights bears the endorsement of a long tradition of open, widespread, and unchallenged use that dates back to the beginning of the Republic, we have no proper basis for striking it down." As this quote suggests, Justice Scalia often wielded existing traditions as a shield, one meant to inhibit the judicial creation of new rights. In certain substantive due process cases, like the dispute over a right to physician-assisted suicide, the absence of a tradition supporting the existence of a right led him to reject the claimed right. Yet there also was the prospect that the Justice would endorse traditional rights that the Court had not previously recognized. With respect to the right to keep and bear arms, arguments from tradition led Justice Scalia to endorse the notion that the right applied against the states. Regarding habeas corpus, the Justice cited tradition repeatedly in declaring that captured citizens who allegedly waged war against the United States had a constitutional right to be released or to be criminally charged.

These four jurisprudential influences sometimes worked in concert, pointing to a single answer. Yet it could not always be so. In *NLRB* v. *Noel Canning*, a broad reading of the Recess Appointments Clause grounded on tradition lost out to the Clause's original meaning. In *McIntyre* v. *Ohio Elections Commission*, though there was a powerful case that the First Amendment protected anonymous political speech, Justice Scalia sided with the progressive tradition that permitted the state to ban anonymous speech. The Justice's penchant for rules sometimes seemed to get the better of his fidelity to the original Constitution; his steadfast refusal to consider whether congressional delegations of vast rulemaking authority were unconstitutional delegations of legislative power comes to mind. Yet when it came to gun rights, originalist readings of the Constitution trumped concerns about judicial restraint. Because Justice Scalia, like most everyone, had multiple commitments, he sometimes was forced to choose amongst them.

The recurrence of certain themes perhaps implied that Justice Scalia regarded other considerations as beyond the pale. But the Justice was not content to leave this conclusion to implication. He was quite vocal about his bêtes noires, those Mephistophelian ideas that he considered infernal. These were devils that he sought to slay on every occasion.

The Justice had at least two black beasts. First, he rejected the claim that the meaning of laws could drift or change without a formal change in text. This opposition made him dead set against the theory of the living Constitution. He was certain that something could not become unconstitutional (or constitutional) merely because political views or moral sensibilities had changed. Hence he liked to exclaim that the Constitution was not living but "dead, dead, dead." Second, and in keeping with his opposition to a living Constitution, the Justice combated the tendency of judges to read their preferences into the law. "Now the main danger in judicial interpretation of the Constitution . . . is that the judges will mistake their own predilections for the law." Judges were meant to be agents, applying law enacted by others. The Constitution never authorized them to impose their own morality under the guise of enforcing those laws.

II. No Apologia

The Justice seemed ever faithful to the principle that the Constitution was dead. I do not believe that he ever discovered a novel right on the grounds that modern morality or society demanded it. Nor do I believe he ever read a right out of the Constitution merely because he thought it had outlived whatever usefulness it might have once had. Whatever legal conclusions the Justice drew, he was apt to say that his reading of the law had always been the right one, whatever the Court might have said in the past. It had not become right with the passage of time or changes in personnel or morality. While perceptions of the law might change, the meaning of a fixed law remained fixed.

Far more challenging was the task of separating judicial preferences from the law. It is difficult to list rulings that ran athwart of his personal convictions because Justices ordinarily do not reveal the latter. Still it seems that Justice Scalia sometimes successfully sidelined his predilections. Though he voted to strike down a state law banning the desecration of the American flag on the grounds that the law was unconstitutional, he apparently wanted to jail "sandal-wearing, scruffy-bearded weirdo[es] who" burnt the flag. His votes in *Crawford* v. *Washington* and *Apprendi* v. *New Jersey* seemed triumphs of originalist principle over policy considerations.

Yet, like the rest of humanity, Justice Scalia was fallible. In thinking about this possibility, reconsider the Justice's enduring devotion to rules, judicial restraint, and traditions. I am inclined to think that it was a misstep for the Justice to give significant, independent weight to these considerations. It is a slip up in the same way that it would be to employ cost-benefit analysis to make educated assessments about optimal constitutional policies and then decree that the Constitution somehow incorporates these policies. It is a blunder in the same way that it is to treat notions of "justice" or the "separation of powers" as freestanding values in constitutional interpretation.

I suppose someone devoted to these values—rules, judicial restraint, traditions—might respond that the Constitution implicitly incorporated them. Assuredly the Constitution does, in the limited sense that particular provisions reflect and embody a respect for tradition or a preference for rules or judicial restraint. But saying that the Constitution is a product of these (and many other) values is different from saying that the Constitution authorizes interpreters to draw upon them as a means of discerning meaning. These values do not appear to permeate every nook and cranny of the Constitution. Nor are they lenses meant to color our reading of the Constitution. Hence a judge who continually refracts the Constitution through these values is apt to acquire a distorted perception, reading standards as rules and imposing restraint where none was imposed.

Despite my mild reproach, I would like to suppose that Justice Scalia came close to the ideal of separating predilection from law. It is easy for the professor to be a purist and insist upon the isolation, and then segregation, of the irrelevant from the relevant. It is far harder for the judge to be so meticulous and unsullied. For the scholar, nothing much of consequence, other than ego, turns on her purity. For the judge, it is much the opposite. A judge's decisions affect flesh and blood. Judges decide whether people may attend school, go to jail, or keep arms.

These continuous encounters with reality, these brushes with the living, help explain why no judge can entirely separate law from predilection. Justice Scalia's humanity perhaps explains why he once admitted to being a "faint-hearted originalist."

Even though he supposed that the Eighth Amendment's original meaning did not ban floggings, he suggested that he would find such beatings unconstitutional. Later, he snatched this concession back, recognizing that it posed a problem, at least for his standing amongst originalists. I was a silent censor, aghast at the concession. But perhaps no one should have to apologize for being human.

Justice Scalia once said that "[t]he judge who always likes the results he reaches is a bad judge." It can equally be said that any jurist who unswervingly sided with the law and steadfastly sidelined personal preferences would not be a human but an angel or automaton. Our benches lack both angels and automatons.

Justice Scalia well understood this last point. He harbored no illusions that judges, originalist or otherwise, would invariably eschew their moral or political preferences. As he put it, "[A] voiding this error [mistaking personal preferences for the law] is the hardest part of being a conscientious judge; perhaps no conscientious judge ever succeeds entirely." On another occasion, he wrote that "[s]ociety's moral beliefs necessarily affect its constitutional perceptions in general . . . . There is no need to apologize for the phenomenon . . . . In any case, it is useless to rail against the phenomenon because it is inevitable." What is true for society in general is no less true for the judges who are part of it. A jurist's moral beliefs necessarily affect her constitutional perceptions.

Nonetheless, there was a marked difference between acknowledging this inevitable weakness and attempting to make a virtue of a vice by applauding judges who yielded to their predilections. Justice Scalia claimed that whereas living constitutionalism nourished and celebrated the judicial proclivity to mistake moral convictions for the law, originalism sought to constrain that tendency, making originalism the lesser evil.

III. Legacy

Justice Scalia was quite influential and will, I predict, remain so. He was not pivotal in the way that Justices Sandra Day O'Connor or Anthony Kennedy often were. After all, he was not often in the middle of the Court. Nor was Justice Scalia influential in the sense that he altered the way the current Justices perceive the Constitution. The approaches of the current Justices were largely shaped long before they ascended to the Supreme Bench. When Professor Greene sets this as a benchmark for influence, he sets a standard too lofty. Good behavior tenure virtually guarantees that no Justice will march to the tune of a colleague, or, for that matter, anyone else. As Brutus put it, federal judges "are independent of the people, of the legislature, and of every power under heaven. Men placed in this situation will generally soon feel themselves independent of heaven itself." The fact that Justices Anthony Kennedy, Stephen Breyer, and many others contested the sometimes enchanting, and sometimes ferocious, arguments of Justice Scalia is neither here nor there, for Justices can resist, contest, or promulgate almost anything.

Justice Scalia was influential in other senses. He changed the Court. His colleagues on the Court knew that they had to gird their opinions with references to text and original meanings, for that would perhaps take some of the sting out of an assertion that they were creating, rather than interpreting, the law. One study found that, within the Supreme Court, Justice Scalia's opinions enjoyed a higher citation rate than those of any other Rehnquist-era Justice, save for Justice John Paul Stevens. His adherence to originalism also altered the way lawyers argue before the Court. Advocates understood that they had to cite the text and make claims about the Constitution's original meaning in their briefs and arguments. Citing precedent and policy arguments was insufficient.

He also swayed those outside the Court. According to Professor Frank Cross, Justice Scalia's opinions issued during a ten-year period on the Rehnquist Court were cited far more frequently by lower courts than those of any other Supreme Court Justice during the same period. Justice Scalia also shaped the course of state constitutional law by helping to usher in jurists with the same bent, like Michigan Supreme Court Justice Joan Larsen. His opinions inspired (or delightfully maddened) students and lawyers, who saw the Justice as either a kindred spirit or a worthy intellectual foil.

In the legal academy, Justice Scalia enjoyed outsized influence. A 2012 ranking of law review articles lists Justice Scalia's The Rule of Law as a Law of Rules as the thirty-sixth most cited article on record. If we tally how many articles were written about Justice Scalia, using that as a proxy for his relative significance, it seems that many scholars were consumed with him. Some 206 articles reference "Scalia" in their titles. This number dwarfs the totals for the other Justices with whom Justice Scalia served over the past two decades.

Justice Scalia's tight embrace of originalism influenced many professors, including Greene. Greene is an extraordinary scholar. Many of his best pieces focus on originalism; he has eight that reference originalism in the title. Can there be a better acknowledgment of originalism's place in the legal academy than a respected scholar like Greene's taking the theory seriously?

To be clear, originalism has not triumphed, for the idea of a living Constitution has not been consigned to the ash heap of history. Yet because originalism has acquired some prominent converts, some scholars hyperbolically claim that "we are all originalists now," and a liberal Justice admitted the same. Theories of the living Constitution seem to be on the back foot.

Was Justice Scalia's time on the bench originalism's high-water mark? Only time will tell. But I think not. Originalism has yet to show signs of faddishness. To the contrary its impact has mushroomed in judicial and circles over the past thirty years. As a new generation of lawyers more thoroughly exposed to originalist thought comes to the fore, it seems likely that originalism will endure. As people continue to advance, defend, refine, and disparage the theory, Justice Scalia's memorable defense of it will remain prominent and extend his influence over originalists and their critics.

Regardless of whether originalism recedes or continues to surge, Justice Scalia will enjoy a richly deserved eminence for the foreseeable future. He was often quotable, in an era when casebooks must condense judicial opinions. He also served as a counterpoint to the sensibilities of most constitutional law professors, thereby providing a useful contrast. Students want a clash of ideas, not a catechism. Finally, Justice Scalia—through his impressive arguments and memorable turns of phrases—inspired many to take up the originalist flag, including thousands of lawyers he barely knew or never met. His opinions, books, and articles guarantee him an enduring sway.

IV. Resistance and Bigotry

As noted, Greene is a keen student of originalism and of Justice Scalia. It is thus strange to see him link originalism to opposition to change, claim that Justice Scalia's agenda consisted of "chronic resistance to novelty," and assert that the Justice's "symbolic purpose was to speak for the law's intolerance of social change." Further, it is puzzling to read that originalism's rivals merely wished for the Constitution "to appear to be open to novel forms of contestation" and favored the "promiscuity of the law." Most discouraging is Greene's openness to the charge that Justice Scalia might have been a bigot.

Greene equates skepticism toward new rights claims to a rearguard action against progress. This is balderdash. Before a court, both parties can easily cast their arguments in the language of rights. Notwithstanding the ancient concept of nuisance, I can claim a novel constitutional right to use my property as I see fit, including a right to emit noxious fumes. In response, my neighbor can assert a constitutional right to be free of such poisonous pollution. In that clash of constitutional rights, is the judge inescapably opposed to social progress? After all, however she rules, the judge will be rejecting a novel constitutional claim. Furthermore, as Judge Robert Bork liked to point out, whenever a litigant asserts a constitutional right against the government, the latter may reply that it seeks to vindicate the right of the majority to legislate. My point is not to belittle novel constitutional rights claims but to underscore that rejection of them cannot be equated to resistance to progress.

Moreover, originalists of Justice Scalia's sort—those that read the Constitution as authorizing judges to enforce but few rights—are not opposed to progress, of any sort. Per the Justice's originalism, the people, through their legislatures, are free to establish or abolish abortion rights. The people are free to establish or abolish the death penalty. And the people are free to establish or abolish the welfare state and the pervasive regulation of private property. In other words, the people are free to make social and moral judgments, revise them over time, and impose them on dissenters. What Justice Scalia combated was the tendency of judges to impose their understandings of social and moral progress on the rest of us or on jurisdictions that stand as outliers.

At some level, all Justices oppose such impositions. If some portion of the judicial right revived the Lochnerian right to contract or held that the Constitution banned abortion, you can bet the house that Justice Ruth Bader Ginsburg would stand in fierce opposition. Even if victorious libertarian pro-lifers insisted that the recognition of their legal claims marked the progress of a maturing society and evolving standards of decency, Justice Ginsburg's recalcitrance could not accurately be equated to hostility to progress. Again, a judge who declines to honor a rights claim should in no way be seen as hostile to progress, social, moral, or otherwise.

As for opponents of originalism, whom Greene calls "pluralis[ts]," undoubtedly there are some who truly desire a robust debate and who would be equanimous in the face of consistent defeat at the hands of judges wedded to multifactor tests and open to novel rights claims. But I imagine that people like Greene are few and far between. A Supreme Court that endorsed newfangled rights and, in the process, overturned *Roe* v. *Wade* or *Wickard* v. *Filburn* would receive little praise from living constitutionalists for being "open to novel forms of contestation" and having embraced "a new constitutional grundnorm of mutual recognition." I suspect that most who endorse living constitutionalism do so because it has been, in the recent past, a successful mechanism for imposing certain aspects of their morality on the entire country. Should living constitutionalism become a consistent means of imposing disfavored moralities, most of its current champions would disdain, rather than esteem, novel rights claims. Most living constitutionalists are of the sunshine varietal.

Finally, a few words about the claim that Justice Scalia's jurisprudence and occasional rhetorical outbursts lent credence to the view that he was bigoted. As evidence, Greene first points to Justice Scalia's treatment of religious freedom. Greene suggests that Justice Scalia, in Employment *Division* v. *Smith*, crafted a rule that disfavored the practices of religious minorities.

Yet in *Burwell* v. *Hobby Lobby Stores, Inc.* Justice Scalia quietly abandoned the harsh rule in order to vindicate the free exercise rights of Christians, or so Greene insinuates.

This charge is off base. The difference between Smith and Hobby Lobby was an intervening congressional statute, the Religious Freedom Restoration Act of 1993 (RFRA) that (re)imposed a tougher, pre-Smith strict scrutiny standard meant to favor free exercise claims. That compelling interest standard protects every religious person, including Hindus, Muslims, and other religious minorities. Justice Scalia well understood this. Consider *Gonzales* v. *O Centro Espirita Beneficente União do Vegetal* from 2006, a case that implemented the RFRA "compelling interest" test. In that case the Justice (and the Court) found that because there was no compelling federal interest justifying the suppression of a hallucinogenic tea, hoasca, members of the União do Vegetal could sip that tea in their rites. Because RFRA was constitutional as applied to the federal government, Justice Scalia (and his colleagues) had to apply the dreaded standard that the Justice had attempted to inter in Smith. Similarly, in Hobby Lobby, every member of the Court agreed about the applicability of the compelling interest test. The simple fact is that Congress rebuffed the Justice's earlier reading of the Free Exercise Clause and found a way of bypassing Smith. In Centro Espirita and in Hobby Lobby, the Justice (and the Court) rightly acquiesced.

Did Justice Scalia's comments about affirmative action in state schools give rise to creditable suspicions of intolerance? Only if one is predisposed to adopt an uncharitable reading of them. People often say things capable of multiple meanings. We would do well not to attribute the worst to those who challenge us. In his essay, Greene chose to take seriously the accusation that Justice Scalia was a bigot. He had the better stance in his *New York Times* piece, where he expressed robust, principled opposition to the Justice's jurisprudence without also lending credence to kooky views.

To Justice Scalia's credit, Greene's criticisms would not have fazed him. Justice Scalia could get annoyed at times, but he had heard far worse. As his former clerk Professor Adrian Vermeule notes, the Justice was courageous in his willingness to stand up for his beliefs, even when it made him unpopular in some quarters. Another clerk, Paul Clement, rightly described the Justice as a "happy warrior." Opponents might say that Justice Scalia was a cretin for originalism and a certain reading of the Constitution. And the Justice, with a beam and twinkle, might bellow, "Yes!" Justice Scalia was a fool for the Constitution and its original meaning, among other things.

> *"The perennial challenge of liberty
> and equality are how to unite
> the goals of freedom and the
> common good."*

Equal Opportunity Ensures Equal Justice

Bill of Rights Institute

In the following viewpoint, authors from the Bill of Rights Institute assert that the Founders' talk of equal opportunity is sufficient to ensure justice for all—even if the framers did not mean for that opportunity to extend to everyone. One of the primary arguments against an originalist interpretation of the Constitution is that if that philosophy were truly adhered to it would be easy to justify denying rights to the vast majority of citizens today. The Bill of Rights Institute is a nonprofit organization that offers education and development on American history and government for youth and teachers.

As you read, consider the following questions:

1. What does *novus ordo seclorum* mean?
2. According to the viewpoint, how did those not originally afforded rights in the Bill of Rights fight to achieve the "American Dream"?
3. Does the viewpoint believe that equal opportunity necessarily results in equal treatment under the law?

When the delegates to the Constitution Convention were preparing to sign the new Constitution, Benjamin Franklin gave a speech to say why his fellow delegates should sign the Constitution. Franklin admitted that it was not a perfect document, and that he had his doubts about some parts of it. Nevertheless, he believed that it was a great framework of government that would protect the liberties of the people and was the best that could be obtained considering that they were fallible men. He and the other Framers affixed their signatures to the great document of freedom because of the promise it had to create a lasting republic on free principles.

It was a unique moment in world history that a scattered and diverse people in America could stop at a critical period to deliberate over a whole new government and the founding of a nation on a core set of principles. The promise of America in the vision of the Founders was that of liberty and equality in the Declaration of Independence and Constitution. The natural rights republic new concept was grounded upon principles that did not change with the passing of time or the changes in culture. This *novus ordo seclorum*—"new order for the ages"—was not created for a particular race, privileged aristocratic social class, or member of an established religion, but for all equally.

With all of the promise of these enduring principles, America was a nation in which African-Americans suffered the horrors of slavery, women could not vote, and Native Americans were roundly denied almost any rights.

> James Madison wrote in Federalist No. 51 that, "Justice is the end of government. It is the end of civil society. It ever has been, and ever will be, pursued, until it be obtained" (James Madison, Federalist No. 51, 1788).

However, these groups were not living under a just government that protected their rights or fulfilled the purposes for which it was created. But, were the principles of natural justice themselves flawed, or were they applied by fallible men?

For nearly two hundred years, African-Americans, women, Native Americans, and other groups have fought to win equal rights by arguing that America should live up to these ideals. They wanted the same right to participate equally in the American political system as citizens and enjoy the "American Dream." They could have rejected that society and its principles for discriminating against them for so long. They could have worked outside the system for radical change or worked to destroy the system as has been done in other countries throughout modern history. However, they consistently appealed to the same principles that animated the Founders in creating the Declaration of Independence and Constitution, and used their right of free speech and freedom of assembly to argue for nothing less than full participation in American society and enjoyment of their equal rights as citizens and humans endowed with inalienable rights.

Even after the many successes the movements for liberty and equality achieved, the debate continued. Today, debates over gay marriage, affirmative action, and economic justice, and the role of the government in resolving these disputes, are still highly contentious. The debates often revolve around different views of what rights are embedded in the natural law as opposed to what might be just commonly held ideas by the majority. At other times, justice can be interpreted as individual conscience applied to society. Is this how the Founders understood natural law or justice? Of course, in any issue, there are contending sides who believe that they are arguing according to a principle. This is why free and open discourse employing reason must guide deliberation in a self-governing society and why reason must trump mere ideology.

> Another change in recent American thinking about issues of diversity, equality, and liberty is a redefinition of idea of equality. The Founding vision equality of opportunity, where all have the same chance to employ their talents and merits, in American politics, economy, and society has been supplanted by an advocacy of an equality of outcomes.

Some believe that equal opportunity is often not enough because there are still those who are more successful than others and thus unequal. All people must be made equal by a government which regulates society and reverses centuries of discrimination by granting special favors to certain groups such as women, African-Americans, and Native Americans. Is this a proper understanding of equality? Does this create a more just society? Are certain groups entitled to special protections and favors by the government? Our republic and its free enterprise economy was founded upon the idea of equality under the law in which all had the same opportunity to pursue their happiness.

America has always been and continues to be a diverse country. One question that will confront all Americans is how to ensure that every citizen, regardless of skin color, sex, or religion, will enjoy the liberty and equality that the country was founded upon. Another question is whether Americans will continue to agree upon the fundamental principles upon which the country was founded and the meaning of those principles or whether we will be fragmented into groups with a narrow perspective and only look out for our own interests. The perennial challenge of liberty and equality are how to unite the goals of freedom and the common good.

> What was so exceptional about the American Founding was that the nation offered an experiment for mankind in liberty and equality.

The Founders did not merely attack monarchy and aristocracy but looked to build a lasting republic on the principles best suited to human nature. They were not merely locked in their time and place in the eighteenth century but were far-seeing statesmen and lawgivers who framed an enduring Constitution for a lasting republic. Rather than evolving or changing with the times, the Constitution had immutable principles that would allow Americans to govern themselves down through the ages. It did not matter for the Founders what the diverse character of the citizenry was, but rather than they embraced the universal principles upon which America was founded.

> *"The genius of the Constitution rests not in any static meaning it might have had in a world that is dead and gone, but in the adaptability of its great principles to cope with current problems and current needs."*

The Ambiguity of the Constitution Requires Interpretation

William J. Brennan

In the following viewpoint, William J. Brennan argues that an originalist approach is "little more than arrogance cloaked as humility." In this transcript of a lecture he delivered at Georgetown University in Washington, DC, many years ago, Brennan began by discussing the values embodied in the Constitution and the weight of the responsibility for interpreting the document. A justice with a very different judicial philosophy from that of Justice Scalia, Brennan also pointed out some of the dangers of a strict interpretation of the Constitution. William J. Brennan Jr. served as a US Supreme Court justice from 1956 to 1990.

"Constitutional Interpretation," by William J. Brennan Jr., Ashbrook Center, October 12, 1985. Reprinted by permission.

As you read, consider the following questions:

1. What word does Brennan use to describe his relation to the Constitution?

2. Why does Brennan say an "unabashed enshrinement of the majority" would lead to the imposition of a social caste system?

3. How have changes in the economic basis of the nation affected the interpretation of law, according to this viewpoint?

It will perhaps not surprise you that the text I have chosen for exploration is the amended Constitution of the United States, which, of course, entrenches the Bill of Rights and the Civil War amendments, and draws sustenance from the bedrock principles of another great text, the Magna Carta. So fashioned, the Constitution embodies the aspiration to social justice, brotherhood, and human dignity that brought this nation into being. The Declaration of Independence, the Constitution and the Bill of Rights solemnly committed the United States to be a country where the dignity and rights of all persons were equal before all authority. In all candor we must concede that part of this egalitarianism in America has been more pretension than realized fact. But we are an aspiring people, a people with faith in progress. Our amended Constitution is the lodestar for our aspirations. Like every text worth reading, it is not crystalline. The phrasing is broad and the limitations of its provisions are not clearly marked. Its majestic generalities and ennobling pronouncements are both luminous and obscure. This ambiguity of course calls forth interpretation, the interaction of reader and text. The encounter with the constitutional text has been, in many senses, my life's work.

My approach to this text may differ from the approach of other participants in this symposium to their texts. Yet such differences may themselves stimulate reflection about what it is we do when we "interpret" a text. Thus I will attempt to elucidate my approach to the text as well as my substantive interpretation.

Perhaps the foremost difference is the fact that my encounters with the constitutional text are not purely or even primarily introspective; the Constitution cannot be for me simply a contemplative haven for private moral reflection. My relation to this great text is inescapably public. That is not to say that my reading of the text is not a personal reading, only that the personal reading perforce occurs in a public context, and is open to critical scrutiny from all quarters.

The Constitution is fundamentally a public text—the monumental charter of a government and a people—and a Justice of the Supreme Court must apply it to resolve public controversies. For, from our beginnings, a most important consequence of the constitutionally created separation of powers has been the American habit, extraordinary to other democracies, of casting social, economic, philosophical and political questions in the form of law suits, in an attempt to secure ultimate resolution by the Supreme Court. In this way, important aspects of the most fundamental issues confronting our democracy may finally arrive in the Supreme Court for judicial determination. Not infrequently, these are the issues upon which contemporary society is most deeply divided. They arouse our deepest emotions. The main burden of my twenty-nine terms on the Supreme Court has thus been to wrestle with the Constitution in this heightened public context, to draw meaning from the text in order to resolve public controversies.

Two other aspects of my relation to this text warrant mention. First, constitutional interpretation for a federal judge is, for the most part, obligatory. When litigants approach the bar of court to adjudicate a constitutional dispute, they may justifiably demand an answer. Judges cannot avoid a definitive interpretation because they feel unable to, or would prefer not to, penetrate to the full meaning of the Constitution's provisions. Unlike literary critics, judges cannot merely savor the tensions or revel in the ambiguities inhering in the text—judges must resolve them.

Second, consequences flow from a justice's interpretation in a direct and immediate way. A judicial decision respecting the incompatibility of Jim Crow with a constitutional guarantee of equality is not simply a contemplative exercise in defining the shape of a just society. It is an order—supported by the full coercive power of the State—that the present society change in a fundamental aspect. Under such circumstances the process of deciding can be a lonely, troubling experience for fallible human beings conscious that their best may not be adequate to the challenge. We Justices are certainly aware that we are not final because we are infallible; we know that we are infallible only because we are final. One does not forget how much may depend on the decision. More than the litigants may be affected. The course of vital social, economic and political currents may be directed.

These three defining characteristics of my relation to the constitutional text—its public nature, obligatory character, and consequentialist aspect—cannot help but influence the way I read that text. When Justices interpret the Constitution they speak for their community, not for themselves alone. The act of interpretation must be undertaken with full consciousness that it is, in a very real sense, the community's interpretation that is sought. Justices are not platonic guardians appointed to wield authority according to their personal moral predilections. Precisely because coercive force must attend any judicial decision to countermand the will of a contemporary majority, the Justices must render constitutional interpretations that are received as legitimate. The source of legitimacy is, of course, a wellspring of controversy in legal and political circles. At the core of the debate is what the late Yale Law School professor Alexander Bickel labeled "the counter—majoritarian difficulty." Our commitment to self—governance in a representative democracy must be reconciled with vesting in electorally unaccountable Justices the power to invalidate the expressed desires of representative bodies on the ground of inconsistency with higher law. Because judicial power resides in the authority to give meaning to the Constitution, the debate is really a debate about how to read the text, about constraints on what is legitimate interpretation.

There are those who find legitimacy in fidelity to what they call "the intentions of the Framers." In its most doctrinaire incarnation, this view demands that Justices discern exactly what the Framers thought about the question under consideration and simply follow that intention in resolving the case before them. It is a view that feigns self—effacing deference to the specific judgments of those who forged our original social compact. But in truth it is little more than arrogance cloaked as humility. It is arrogant to pretend that from our vantage we can gauge accurately the intent of the Framers on application of principle to specific, contemporary questions. All too often, sources of potential enlightment such as records of the ratification debates provide sparse or ambiguous evidence of the original intention. Typically, all that can be gleaned is that the Framers themselves did not agree about the application or meaning of particular constitutional provisions, and hid their differences in cloaks of generality. Indeed, it is far from clear whose intention is relevant—that of the drafters, the congressional disputants, or the ratifiers in the states?—or even whether the idea of an original intention is a coherent way of thinking about a jointly drafted document drawing its authority from a general assent of the states. And apart from the problematic nature of the sources, our distance of two centuries cannot but work as a prism refracting all we perceive. One cannot help but speculate that the chorus of lamentations calling for interpretation faithful to "original intention"—and proposing nullification of interpretations that fail this quick litmus test—must inevitably come from persons who have no familiarity with the historical record.

Perhaps most importantly, while proponents of this facile historicism justify it as a depoliticization of the judiciary, the political underpinnings of such a choice should not escape notice. A position that upholds constitutional claims only if they were within the specific contemplation of the Framers in effect establishes a presumption of resolving textual ambiguities against the claim of constitutional right. It is far from clear what justifies such a presumption against claims of right. Nothing intrinsic in the nature of interpretation—if there is such a thing as the "nature" of interpretation—commands such a passive approach to ambiguity. This is a choice no less political than any other; it expresses antipathy to claims of the minority rights against the majority. Those who would restrict claims of right to the values of 1789 specifically articulated in the Constitution turn a blind eye to social progress and eschew adaptation of overarching principles to changes of social circumstance.

Another, perhaps more sophisticated, response to the potential power of judicial interpretation stresses democratic theory: because ours is a government of the people's elected representatives, substantive value choices should by and large be left to them. This view emphasizes not the transcendent historical authority of the framers but the predominant contemporary authority of the elected branches of government. Yet it has similar consequences for the nature of proper judicial interpretation. Faith in the majoritarian process counsels restraint. Even under more expansive formulations of this approach, judicial review is appropriate only to the extent of ensuring that our democratic process functions smoothly. Thus, for example, we would protect freedom of speech merely to ensure that the people are heard by their representatives, rather than as a separate, substantive value. When, by contrast, society tosses up to the Supreme Court a dispute that would require invalidation of a legislature's substantive policy choice, the Court generally would stay its hand because the Constitution was meant as a plan of government and not as an embodiment of fundamental substantive values.

The view that all matters of substantive policy should be resolved through the majoritarian process has appeal under some circumstances, but I think it ultimately will not do. Unabashed enshrinement of majority will would permit the imposition of a social caste system or wholesale confiscation of property so long as a majority of the authorized legislative body, fairly elected, approved. Our Constitution could not abide such a situation. It is the very purpose of a Constitution—and particularly of the Bill of Rights—to declare certain values transcendent, beyond the reach of temporary political majorities. The majoritarian process cannot be expected to rectify claims of minority right that arise as a response to the outcomes of that very majoritarian process. As James Madison put it:

> The prescriptions in favor of liberty ought to be leveled against that quarter where the greatest danger lies, namely, that which possesses the highest prerogative of power. But this is not found in either the Executive or Legislative departments of Government, but in the body of the people, operating by the majority against the minority. (I Annals 437).

Faith in democracy is one thing, blind faith quite another. Those who drafted our Constitution understood the difference. One cannot read the text without admitting that it embodies substantive value choices; it places certain values beyond the power of any legislature. Obvious are the separation of powers; the privilege of the Writ of Habeas Corpus; prohibition of Bills of Attainder and *ex post facto* laws; prohibition of cruel and unusual punishments; the requirement of just compensation for official taking of property; the prohibition of laws tending to establish religion or enjoining the free exercise of religion; and, since the Civil War, the banishment of slavery and official race discrimination. With respect to at least such principles, we simply have not constituted ourselves as strict utilitarians. While the Constitution may be amended, such amendments require an immense effort by the People as a whole.

To remain faithful to the content of the Constitution, therefore, an approach to interpreting the text must account for the existence of these substantive value choices, and must accept the ambiguity inherent in the effort to apply them to modern circumstances. The Framers discerned fundamental principles through struggles against particular malefactions of the Crown; the struggle shapes the particular contours of the articulated principles. But our acceptance of the fundamental principles has not and should not bind us to those precise, at times anachronistic, contours. Successive generations of Americans have continued to respect these fundamental choices and adopt them as their own guide to evaluating quite different historical practices. Each generation has the choice to overrule or add to the fundamental principles enunciated by the Framers; the Constitution can be amended or it can be ignored. Yet with respect to its fundamental principles, the text has suffered neither fate. Thus, if I may borrow the words of an esteemed predecessor, Justice Robert Jackson, the burden of judicial interpretation is to translate "the majestic generalities of the Bill of Rights, conceived as part of the pattern of liberal government in the eighteenth century, into concrete restraints on officials dealing with the problems of the twentieth century." *Board of Education* v. *Barnette*, [319 US 624, 639 (1943),] We current Justices read the Constitution in the only way that we can: as Twentieth Century Americans. We look to the history of the time of framing and to the intervening history of interpretation. But the ultimate question must be, what do the words of the text mean in our time. For the genius of the Constitution rests not in any static meaning it might have had in a world that is dead and gone, but in the adaptability of its great principles to cope with current problems and current needs. What the constitutional fundamentals meant to the wisdom of other times cannot be their measure to the vision of our time. Similarly, what those fundamentals mean for us, our descendants will learn, cannot be the measure to the vision of their time. This realization is not, I assure you, a novel one of my own creation. Permit me to quote from one of the opinions of our Court, *Weems* v. *United States,* [217 US 349,] written nearly a century ago:

> Time works changes, brings into existence new conditions and purposes. Therefore, a principle to be vital must be capable of wider application than the mischief which gave it birth. This is peculiarly true of constitutions. They are not ephemeral enactments, designed to meet passing occasions. They are, to use

the words of Chief Justice John Marshall, 'designed to approach immortality as nearly as human institutions can approach it.' The future is their care and provision or events of good and bad tendencies of which no prophesy can be made. In the application of a constitution, therefore, our contemplation cannot be only of what has been, but of what may be.

Interpretation must account for the transformative purpose of the text. Our Constitution was not intended to preserve a preexisting society but to make a new one, to put in place new principles that the prior political community had not sufficiently recognized. Thus, for example, when we interpret the Civil War Amendments to the charter—abolishing slavery, guaranteeing blacks equality under law, and guaranteeing blacks the right to vote—we must remember that those who put them in place had no desire to enshrine the status quo. Their goal was to make over their world, to eliminate all vestige of slave caste.

Having discussed at some length how I, as a Supreme Court Justice, interact with this text, I think it time to turn to the fruits of this discourse. For the Constitution is a sublime oration on the dignity of man, a bold commitment by a people to the ideal of libertarian dignity protected through law. Some reflection is perhaps required before this can be seen.

The Constitution on its face is, in large measure, a structuring text, a blueprint for government. And when the text is not prescribing the form of government it is limiting the powers of that government. The original document, before addition of any of the amendments, does not speak primarily of the rights of man, but of the abilities and disabilities of government. When one reflects upon the text's preoccupation with the scope of government as well as its shape, however, one comes to understand that what this text is about is the relationship of the individual and the state. The text marks the metes and bounds of official authority and individual autonomy. When one studies the boundary that the text marks out, one gets a sense of the vision of the individual embodied in the Constitution.

As augmented by the Bill of Rights and the Civil War Amendments, this text is a sparkling vision of the supremacy of the human dignity of every individual. This vision is reflected in the very choice of democratic self—governance: the supreme value of a democracy is the presumed worth of each individual. And this vision manifests itself most dramatically in the specific prohibitions of the Bill of Rights, a term which I henceforth will apply to describe not only the original first eight amendments, but the Civil War amendments as well. It is a vision that has guided us as a people throughout our history, although the precise rules by which we have protected fundamental human dignity have been transformed over time in response to both transformations of social condition and evolution of our concepts of human dignity.

Until the end of the nineteenth century, freedom and dignity in our country found meaningful protection in the institution of real property. In a society still largely agricultural, a piece of land provided men not just with sustenance but with the means of economic independence, a necessary precondition of political independence and expression. Not surprisingly, property relationships formed the heart of litigation and of legal practice, and lawyers and judges tended to think stable property relationships the highest aim of the law.

But the days when common law property relationships dominated litigation and legal practice are past. To a growing extent economic existence now depends on less certain relationships with government—licenses, employment, contracts, subsidies, unemployment benefits, tax exemptions, welfare and the like. Government participation in the economic existence of individuals is pervasive and deep. Administrative matters and other dealings with government are at the epicenter of the exploding law. We turn to government and to the law for controls which would never have been expected or tolerated before this century, when a man's answer to economic oppression or difficulty was to move two hundred miles west. Now hundreds of thousands of Americans live entire lives without any real prospect of the dignity and autonomy that ownership of real property could confer. Protection of the human dignity of such citizens requires a much modified view of the proper relationship of individual and state.

In general, problems of the relationship of the citizen with government have multiplied and thus have engendered some of the most important constitutional issues of the day. As government acts ever more deeply upon those areas of our lives once marked "private," there is an even greater need to see that individual rights are not curtailed or cheapened in the interest of what may temporarily appear to be the "public good." And as government continues in its role of provider for so many of our disadvantaged citizens, there is an even greater need to ensure that government act with integrity and consistency in its dealings with these citizens. To put this another way, the possibilities for collision between government activity and individual rights will increase as the power and authority of government itself expands, and this growth, in turn, heightens the need for constant vigilance at the collision points. If our free society is to endure, those who govern must recognize human dignity and accept the enforcement of constitutional limitations on their power conceived by the Framers to be necessary to preserve that dignity and the air of freedom which is our proudest heritage. Such recognition will not come from a technical understanding of the organs of government, or the new forms of wealth they administer. It requires something different, something deeper—a personal confrontation with the well—springsof our society. Solutions of constitutional questions from that perspective have become the great challenge of the modern era. All the talk in the last half—decade about shrinking the government does not alter this reality or the challenge it imposes. The modern activist state is a concomitant of the complexity of modern society; it is inevitably with us. We must meet the challenge rather than wish it were not before us.

The challenge is essentially, of course, one to the capacity of our constitutional structure to foster and protect the freedom, the dignity, and the rights of all persons within our borders, which it is the great design of the Constitution to secure. During the time of my public service this challenge has largely taken shape within the confines of the interpretive question whether the specific guarantees of the Bill of Rights operate as restraints on the power of State government. We recognize the Bill of Rights as the primary source of express information as to what is meant by constitutional liberty. The safeguards enshrined in it are deeply etched in the foundation of America's freedoms. Each is a protection with centuries of history behind it, often dearly bought with the blood and lives of people determined to prevent oppression by their rulers. The first eight Amendments, however, were added to the Constitution to operate solely against federal power. It was not until the Thirteenth and Fourteenth Amendments were added, in 1865 and 1868, in response to a demand for national protection against abuses of state power, that the Constitution could be interpreted to require application of the first eight amendments to the states.

It was in particular the Fourteenth Amendment's guarantee that no person be deprived of life, liberty or property without process of law that led us to apply many of the specific guarantees of the Bill of Rights to the States. In my judgment, Justice Cardozo best captured the reasoning that brought us to such decisions when he described what the Court has done as a process by which the guarantees "have been taken over from the earlier articles of the federal bill of rights and brought within the Fourteenth Amendment by a process of absorption ... [that] has had its source in the belief that neither liberty nor justice would exist if [those guarantees] ... were sacrificed." *Palko* v. *Connecticut*, [302 US 319, 326 (1937),]. But this process of absorption was neither swift nor steady. As late as 1922 only the Fifth Amendment guarantee of just compensation for official taking of property had been given force against the states. Between then and 1956 only the First Amendment guarantees of speech and conscience and the Fourth Amendment ban of unreasonable searches and seizures had been incorporated—the latter, however, without the exclusionary rule to give it force. As late as 1961, I could stand before a distinguished assemblage of the bar at New York University's James Madison Lecture and list the following as guarantees that had not been thought to be sufficiently fundamental to the protection of human dignity so as to be enforced against the states: the prohibition of cruel and unusual punishments, the right against self—incrimination, the right to assistance of counsel in a criminal trial, the right to confront witnesses, the right to compulsory process, the right not to be placed in jeopardy of life or limb more than once upon accusation of a crime, the right not to have illegally obtained evidence introduced at a criminal trial, and the right to a jury of one's peers.

The history of the quarter century following that Madison Lecture need not be told in great detail. Suffice it to say that each of the guarantees listed above has been recognized as a fundamental aspect of ordered liberty. Of course, the above catalogue encompasses only the rights of the criminally accused, those caught, rightly or wrongly, in the maw of the criminal justice system. But it has been well said that there is no better test of a society than how it treats those accused of transgressing against it. Indeed, it is because we recognize that incarceration strips a man of his dignity that we demand strict adherence to fair procedure and proof of guilt beyond a reasonable doubt before taking such a drastic step. These requirements are, as Justice Harlan once said, "bottomed on a fundamental value determination of our society that it is far worse to convict an innocent man than to let a guilty man go free." *In re Winship*, [397 US 358, 372 (1970),] (concurring opinion). There is no worse injustice than wrongly to strip a man of his dignity. And our adherence to the constitutional vision of human dignity is so strict that even after convicting a person according to these stringent standards, we demand that his dignity be infringed only to the extent appropriate to the crime and never by means of wanton infliction of pain or deprivation. I interpret the Constitution plainly to embody these fundamental values.

Of course the constitutional vision of human dignity has, in this past quarter century, infused far more than our decisions about the criminal process. Recognition of the principle of "one person, one vote" as a constitutional one redeems the promise of self—governance by affirming the essential dignity of every citizen in the right to equal participation in the democratic process. Recognition of so—called "new property" rights in those receiving government entitlements affirms the essential dignity of the least fortunate among us by demanding that government treat with decency, integrity and consistency those dependent on its benefits for their very survival. After all, a legislative majority initially decides to create governmental entitlements; the Constitution's Due Process Clause merely provides protection for entitlements thought necessary by society as a whole. Such due process rights prohibit government from imposing the devil's bargain of bartering away human dignity in exchange for human sustenance. Likewise, recognition of full equality for women—equal protection of the laws—ensures that gender has no bearing on claims to human dignity.

Recognition of broad and deep rights of expression and of con" science reaffirm the vision of human dignity in many ways. They too redeem the promise of self—governance by facilitating—indeed demanding—robust, uninhibited and wide—open debate on issues of public importance. Such public debate is of course vital to the development and dissemination of political ideas. As importantly, robust public discussion is the crucible in which personal political convictions are forged. In our democracy, such discussion is a political duty, it is the essence of self government. The constitutional vision of human dignity rejects the possibility of political orthodoxy imposed from above; it respects the right of each individual to form and to express political judgments, however far they may deviate from the mainstream and however unsettling they might be to the powerful or the elite. Recognition of these rights of expression and conscience also frees up the private space for both intellectual and spiritual development free of government dominance, either blatant or subtle. Justice Brandeis put it so well sixty years ago when he wrote: "Those who won our independence believed that the final end of the State was to make men free to develop their faculties; and that in its government the deliberative forces should prevail over the arbitrary. They valued liberty both as an end and as a means." *Whitney* v. *California* [274 US 357, 375 (1927),] (concurring opinion).

I do not mean to suggest that we have in the last quarter century achieved a comprehensive definition of the constitutional ideal of human dignity. We are still striving toward that goal, and doubtless it will be an eternal quest. For if the interaction of this Justice and the constitutional text over the years confirms any single proposition, it is that the demands of human dignity will never cease to evolve.

Indeed, I cannot in good conscience refrain from mention of one grave and crucial respect in which we continue, in my judgment, to fall short of the constitutional vision of human dignity. It is in our continued tolerance of State—administered execution as a form of punishment. I make it a practice not to comment on the constitutional issues that come before the Court, but my position on this issue, of course, has been for some time fixed and immutable. I think I can venture some thoughts on this particular subject without transgressing my usual guideline too severely.

As I interpret the Constitution, capital punishment is under all circumstances cruel and unusual punishment prohibited by the Eighth and Fourteenth Amendments. This is a position of which I imagine you are not unaware. Much discussion of the merits of capital punishment has in recent years focused on the potential arbitrariness that attends its administration, and I have no doubt that such arbitrariness is a grave wrong. But for me, the wrong of capital punishment transcends such procedural issues. As I have said in my opinions, I view the Eighth Amendment's prohibition of cruel and unusual punishments as embodying to a unique degree moral principles that substantively restrain the punishments our civilized society may impose on those persons who transgress its laws. Foremost among the moral principles recognized in our cases and inherent in the prohibition is the primary principle that the State, even as it punishes, must treat its citizens in a manner consistent with their intrinsic worth as human beings. A punishment must not be so severe as to be utterly and irreversibly degrading to the very essence of human dignity. Death for whatever crime and under all circumstances is a truly awesome punishment. The calculated killing of a human being by the State involves, by its very nature, an absolute denial of the executed person's humanity. The most vile murder does not, in my view, release the State from constitutional restraints on the destruction of human dignity. Yet an executed person has lost the very right to have rights, now or ever. For me, then, the fatal constitutional infirmity of capital punishment is that it treats members of the human race as nonhumans, as objects to be toyed with and discarded. It is, indeed, "cruel and unusual." It is thus inconsistent with the fundamental premise of the Clause that even the most base criminal remains a human being possessed of some potential, at least, for common human dignity.

This is an interpretation to which a majority of my fellow Justices—not to mention, it would seem, a majority of my fellow countrymen—does not subscribe. Perhaps you find my adherence to it, and my recurrent publication of it, simply contrary, tiresome, or quixotic. Or perhaps you see in it a refusal to abide by the judicial principle of *stare decisis*, obedience to precedent. In my judgment, however, the unique interpretive role of the Supreme Court with respect to the Constitution demands some flexibility with respect to the call of *stare decisis*. Because we are the last word on the meaning of the Constitution, our views must be subject to revision over time, or the Constitution falls captive, again, to the anachronistic views of long—gone generations. I mentioned earlier the judge's role in seeking out the community's interpretation of the Constitutional text. Yet, again in my judgment, when a Justice perceives an interpretation of the text to have departed so far from its essential meaning, that Justice is bound, by a larger constitutional duty to the community, to expose the departure and point toward a different path. On this issue, the death penalty, I hope to embody a community striving for human dignity for all, although perhaps not yet arrived.

You have doubtless observed that this description of my personal encounter with the constitutional text has in large portion been a discussion of public developments in constitutional doctrine over the last century. That, as I suggested at the outset, is inevitable because my interpretive career has demanded a public reading of the text. This public encounter with the text, however, has been a profound source of personal inspiration. The vision of human dignity embodied there is deeply moving. It is timeless. It has inspired Americans for two centuries and it will continue to inspire as it continues to evolve. That evolutionary process is inevitable and indeed, it is the true interpretive genius of the text.

If we are to be as a shining city upon a hill, it will be because of our ceaseless pursuit of the constitutional ideal of human dignity. For the political and legal ideals that form the foundation of much that is best in American institutions—ideals jealously preserved and guarded throughout our history—still form the vital force in creative political thought and activity within the nation today. As we adapt our institutions to the ever-changing conditions of national and international life, those ideals of human dignity—liberty and justice for all individuals—will continue to inspire and guide u because they are entrenched in our Constitution. The Constitution with its Bill of Rights thus has a bright future, as well as a glorious past, for its spirit is inherent in the aspirations of our people.

Periodical and Internet Sources Bibliography

The following articles have been selected to supplement the diverse views presented in this chapter.

Saul Cornell, "New Originalism: A Constitutional Scam," *Dissent*, May 3, 2011. https://www.dissentmagazine.org/online_articles/new-originalism-a-constitutional-scam.

Joseph J. Ellis "Immaculate Conception and the Supreme Court," *Washington Post*, May 7, 2010. http://www.washingtonpost.com/wp-dyn/content/article/2010/05/02/AR2010050202446.html.

Garrett Epps, "Constitutional Myth #1: The Right Is 'Originalist,' Everyone Else Is 'Idiotic,'" *Atlantic*, May 25, 2011. https://www.theatlantic.com/national/archive/2011/05/constitutional-myth-1-the-right-is-originalist-everyone-else-is-idiotic/239291/.

Richard A. Posner, "The Incoherence of Antonin Scalia," *New Republic*, August 23, 2012. https://newrepublic.com/article/106441/scalia-garner-reading-the-law-textual-.

Jeffrey Rosen, "Interpreting the Constitution in the Digital Era," *Fresh Air*, National Public Radio, November 30, 2011. https://www.npr.org/2011/11/30/142714568/interpreting-the-constitution-in-the-digital-era.

Ilya Shapiro, "Amending Justice Stevens: How and Why We Shouldn't Change the Constitution Like This," *Forbes*, April 23, 2014. https://www.forbes.com/sites/ilyashapiro/2014/04/23/amending-justice-stevens-how-and-why-we-shouldnt-change-the-constitution-like-this/#57d4d2174962.

Howard Slugh, "Antonin Scalia: The Forward Looking Justice, *National Review*, February 23, 2016. http://www.nationalreview.com/article/431795/antonin-scalias-originalism-why-critics-are-wrong.

Edward Whelan, "*Brown* and Originalism," *National Review*, May 11, 2005. http://www.nationalreview.com/article/214410/brown-and-originalism-edward-whelan.

George F. Will, "Gorsuch May Be Right Where Scalia Was Wrong," *Salt Lake City Tribune*, February 1, 2017. http://archive.sltrib.com/article.php?id=4891701&itype=CMSID.

CHAPTER 3

Should Justices Exercise Judicial Restraint in Interpreting the Bill of Rights?

Chapter Preface

Whatever their judicial philosophy, judges face a dilemma when it comes to interpreting laws. The Constitution of the United States clearly outlines the roles of the three branches. The legislative branch is meant to make laws and the executive branch to implement and enforce those laws. However, in the Court's responsibility for judicial review, it is often accused of usurping the power of the legislative branch and actually making law. Judicial restraint is the notion that the Court should, whenever possible, bow to the will of the legislative branch, nullifying laws only in rare circumstances. This seems perfectly in keeping with the idea of a democracy ruled by the majority. However, the Constitution, and particularly the Bill of Rights, is also very much concerned with the protection of individuals *from* their government and, by extension, from majorities that rule in that government. When the Court moves to check a government (whether the legislative or the executive branch) that has overstepped the authority given to it by the Constitution, it may in fact be overruling the will of the majority in order to protect the Constitutionally enshrined rights of an individual or of a minority group. Based on a close reading of the Bill of Rights, it seems that this would not be controversial—even if the particulars of a given case might be. However these issues can be, and often are, subject to political whims and oscillations.

At any given time in history, it can seem as if the idea of judicial restraint closely matches a particular party or political position. But it is in fact not always clear which approach benefits what political positions. People who favor judicial restraint in one situation might be perfectly comfortable with what might be called an activist court in another situation. In this chapter, we will take a look at varying viewpoints on the notion of judicial restraint versus judicial activism, and the how these interpretations came to be.

> *"The unique position of the Supreme Court stems, in large part, from the deep commitment of the American people to the Rule of Law and to constitutional government."*

The Court's Responsibility for Judicial Review Protects the Constitution

Supreme Court of the United States

The following viewpoint comes from the website of the Supreme Court of the United States. The authors look at the Bill of Rights from a larger perspective. The viewpoint opens by pointing out that the US Supreme Court is rare in the world in its role as the final arbiter of the nation's laws. It then explains how the Constitution set up three equal branches of government, and looks at the role of the Court in this delicate balance.

As you read, consider the following questions:
1. According to this viewpoint, what is unique about the United States Supreme Court?
2. What Supreme Court decision established judicial review?
3. What, according to this viewpoint, was the precedent for judicial review?

"The Court and Constitutional Interpretation," Supreme Court of the United States.

"Equal Justice Under Law"—These words, written above the main entrance to the Supreme Court Building, express the ultimate responsibility of the Supreme Court of the United States. The Court is the highest tribunal in the Nation for all cases and controversies arising under the Constitution or the laws of the United States. As the final arbiter of the law, the Court is charged with ensuring the American people the promise of equal justice under law and, thereby, also functions as guardian and interpreter of the Constitution.

The Supreme Court is "distinctly American in concept and function," as Chief Justice Charles Evans Hughes observed. Few other courts in the world have the same authority of constitutional interpretation and none have exercised it for as long or with as much influence. A century and a half ago, the French political observer Alexis de Tocqueville noted the unique position of the Supreme Court in the history of nations and of jurisprudence. "The representative system of government has been adopted in several states of Europe," he remarked, "but I am unaware that any nation of the globe has hitherto organized a judicial power in the same manner as the Americans. . . . A more imposing judicial power was never constituted by any people."

The unique position of the Supreme Court stems, in large part, from the deep commitment of the American people to the Rule of Law and to constitutional government. The United States has demonstrated an unprecedented determination to preserve and protect its written Constitution, thereby providing the American "experiment in democracy" with the oldest written Constitution still in force.

The Constitution of the United States is a carefully balanced document. It is designed to provide for a national government sufficiently strong and flexible to meet the needs of the republic, yet sufficiently limited and just to protect the guaranteed rights of citizens; it permits a balance between society's need for order and the individual's right to freedom. To assure these ends, the Framers of the Constitution created three independent and coequal branches of government. That this Constitution has provided continuous democratic government through the periodic stresses of more than two centuries illustrates the genius of the American system of government.

The complex role of the Supreme Court in this system derives from its authority to invalidate legislation or executive actions which, in the Court's considered judgment, conflict with the Constitution. This power of "judicial review" has given the Court a crucial responsibility in assuring individual rights, as well as in maintaining a "living Constitution" whose broad provisions are continually applied to complicated new situations.

While the function of judicial review is not explicitly provided in the Constitution, it had been anticipated before the adoption of that document. Prior to 1789, state courts had already overturned legislative acts which conflicted with state constitutions. Moreover, many of the Founding Fathers expected the Supreme Court to assume this role in regard to the Constitution; Alexander Hamilton and James Madison, for example, had underlined the importance of judicial review in the *Federalist Papers*, which urged adoption of the Constitution.

Hamilton had written that through the practice of judicial review the Court ensured that the will of the whole people, as expressed in their Constitution, would be supreme over the will of a legislature, whose statutes might express only the temporary will of part of the people. And Madison had written that constitutional interpretation must be left to the reasoned judgment of independent judges, rather than to the tumult and conflict of the political process. If every constitutional question were to be decided by public political bargaining, Madison argued, the Constitution would be reduced to a battleground of competing factions, political passion and partisan spirit.

Despite this background the Court's power of judicial review was not confirmed until 1803, when it was invoked by Chief Justice John Marshall in *Marbury* v. *Madison*. In this decision, the Chief Justice asserted that the Supreme Court's responsibility to overturn unconstitutional legislation was a necessary consequence of its sworn duty to uphold the Constitution. That oath could not be fulfilled any other way. "It is emphatically the province of the judicial department to say what the law is," he declared.

In retrospect, it is evident that constitutional interpretation and application were made necessary by the very nature of the Constitution. The Founding Fathers had wisely worded that document in rather general terms leaving it open to future elaboration to meet changing conditions. As Chief Justice Marshall noted in *McCulloch* v. *Maryland*, a constitution that attempted to detail every aspect of its own application "would partake of the prolixity of a legal code, and could scarcely be embraced by the human mind. . . . Its nature, therefore, requires that only its great outlines should be marked, its important objects designated, and the minor ingredients which compose those objects be deduced from the nature of the objects themselves."

The Constitution limits the Court to dealing with "Cases" and "Controversies." John Jay, the first Chief Justice, clarified this restraint early in the Court's history by declining to advise President George Washington on the constitutional implications of a proposed foreign policy decision. The Court does not give advisory opinions; rather, its function is limited only to deciding specific cases.

The Justices must exercise considerable discretion in deciding which cases to hear, since approximately 7,000-8,000 civil and criminal cases are filed in the Supreme Court each year from the various state and federal courts. The Supreme Court also has "original jurisdiction" in a very small number of cases arising out of disputes between States or between a State and the Federal Government.

When the Supreme Court rules on a constitutional issue, that judgment is virtually final; its decisions can be altered only by the rarely used procedure of constitutional amendment or by a new ruling of the Court. However, when the Court interprets a statute, new legislative action can be taken.

Chief Justice Marshall expressed the challenge which the Supreme Court faces in maintaining free government by noting: "We must never forget that it is a constitution we are expounding . . . intended to endure for ages to come, and consequently, to be adapted to the various crises of human affairs."

> *"But the Marbury Court did not claim that the courts possessed the exclusive or supreme authority to interpret the constitutionality of laws. The other branches of government are also legitimately responsible for interpreting the Constitution."*

The Legislative and Executive Branches Have Ceded Too Much Power to the Courts

Robert Alt

In the following viewpoint, Robert Alt argues that the US Supreme Court has the power to interpret law, but not the exclusive power to do so. While many debate the approaches to judicial interpretation, others are concerned that the Court is overstepping its authority and making law rather than strictly interpreting it. The political branches (the legislative and the executive) have willingly ceded this power to the Court, says Alt, and allowed the Court to intervene in what should be political decisions. Robert Alt was a director in the Center for Legal and Judicial Studies, serving under former US attorney general Edwin Meese III at The Heritage Foundation, where he regularly advised members of Congress and Supreme Court litigants on complex legal arguments and strategy.

"What Is the Proper Role of the Courts?" by Robert Alt, The Heritage Foundation, January 20, 2012. Reprinted by permission.

As you read, consider the following questions:

1. According to the article, what motivated the framers to establish separate but equal branches of government?

2. What example does Alt give of President Thomas Jefferson accepting the responsibility for following what he believed was the correct interpretation of the Constitution?

3. What corrective does Alt suggest for courts that are overstepping their authority?

In the *Federalist Papers*, Alexander Hamilton referred to the judiciary as the least dangerous branch of government, stating that judges under the Constitution would possess "neither force nor will, but merely judgment." Yet recently, the courts have wielded great power, directing the President on questions as monumental as how to conduct war, and micromanaging the states concerning even the most minute details of local school and prison operations. What is the proper role of the courts?

> [T]he accumulation of all powers, legislative, executive, and judiciary, in the same hands, whether of one, a few, or many, and whether hereditary, self-appointed, or elective, may justly be pronounced the very definition of tyranny.
>
> —James Madison, Federalist 47

The Founders studied political philosophy and the rise and fall of nations throughout history. When confronted with tyranny on their own shores, they rebelled against the dangerous consolidation of power in the British monarchy. Through reason and experience, they recognized that government can threaten liberty by abusing its powers, and they sought to avoid this by separating powers in the US federal government. They believed that this separation of powers, coupled with a system of checks and balances, would make "ambition … counteract ambition." Rather than depending on officeholders to restrain themselves (which given the power of ambition is unsafe), or on rules set down on paper (which are too easily ignored), the Founders gave each branch authority to exercise, and an interest in defending its own prerogatives, and thereby limited the ability of any one branch to usurp power.

Accordingly, the Founders vested the legislative power (the power to make the laws) in Congress, the executive power (the power to enforce the laws) in the President, and the judicial power (the power to interpret the laws and decide concrete factual cases) with the courts. But even these powers were not unfettered. Federal courts, for example, can hear only "cases or controversies": they cannot issue advisory opinions. The courts cannot expound on a law of their choosing or at the request of even the President himself, but must wait for a genuine case between actual aggrieved parties to be properly presented to the court.

In explaining judicial power under the Constitution, Hamilton noted that the courts would have the authority to determine whether laws passed by the legislature were consistent with the fundamental and superior law of the Constitution. If a law was contrary to the Constitution, then it was void. Not surprisingly, the Supreme Court agreed, famously announcing its authority to rule on the validity of laws—known as judicial review—in the case of *Marbury* v. *Madison*. In weighing the validity of a provision of the Judiciary Act of 1789, Chief Justice John Marshall declared that "It is emphatically the province and duty of the judicial department to say what the law is."

> Those who framed the Constitution chose their words carefully; they debated at great length the most minute points. The language they chose meant something. It is incumbent upon the Court to determine what that meaning was.
>
> —Attorney General Edwin Meese, July 9, 1985

But the *Marbury* Court did not claim that the courts possessed the exclusive or supreme authority to interpret the constitutionality of laws. The other branches of government are also legitimately responsible for interpreting the Constitution. The President, for example, takes an oath to support the Constitution, and carries out this oath by determining which laws to sign. While the President may sign or veto legislation for political or policy reasons, the President faithfully discharges his oath by vetoing legislation if he believes that it would violate the Constitution. If the law was signed by one of his predecessors, a President may engage in constitutional interpretation by choosing not to enforce it if he believes it to be unconstitutional.

Thus, President Thomas Jefferson ordered his Attorney General not to enforce the Alien and Sedition Acts because he believed that they violated the First Amendment. Jefferson did this even though some courts had held that the Acts were constitutional. Jefferson's action is an early practical example of the President using his independent role and judgment to interpret the Constitution.

Members of Congress also take an oath to support the Constitution. Congress interprets the Constitution by deciding which laws to enact. Congress may (and does) choose to enact or reject legislation for political or policy reasons, but when its Members reject legislation that would violate the Constitution, they are acting in accordance with their oaths.

That is how our system is supposed to work. But over time, the Supreme Court has grabbed power by declaring that "the federal judiciary is supreme in the exposition of the law of the Constitution." The Supreme Court has even gone so far as to declare that its decisions that interpret the Constitution are the supreme law of the land.

Unfortunately, the political branches have largely acceded to these bloated claims. For example, when Congress was considering the Bipartisan Campaign Reform Act—popularly known as McCain-Feingold—which imposed numerous restrictions on election-related speech, its Members delivered speeches acknowledging that provisions of the Act were likely unconstitutional. That should have ended the debate.

But some Members surprisingly went on to state that questions of constitutionality were for the Supreme Court, not Congress, to decide, and that Congress should pass the legislation because it was too important not to enact. This was a flagrant abdication of Congress's role in determining the constitutionality of legislation.

Similarly, when President George W. Bush signed the legislation, he issued a statement asserting that he expected the courts to resolve his "reservations about the constitutionality" of provisions of the Act. This once again left the courts to answer constitutional questions that the President could have and should have decided himself. Thus, by the acquiescence of Congress and the President, the weakest branch has largely succeeded in its self-anointed claim of supremacy.

The federal courts have not only grabbed power. They have also changed how judges carry out one of the core function of the judiciary: interpreting laws. The proper role of a judge in a constitutional republic is a modest one. Ours is a government of laws and not men. This basic truth requires that disputes be adjudicated based on what the law actually says, rather than the whims of judges.

In determining whether a contested law is consistent with the Constitution, judges act within their proper judicial power when they give effect to the original public meaning of the words of the law and the Constitution. This necessarily means that judges acting in accordance with their constitutional duties will at times uphold laws that may be bad policy, and strike down laws that may be good policy. This is because judicial review requires the judge to determine not whether the law leads to good or bad results, but whether the law violates the Constitution.

In recent decades, judges have engaged in judicial activism, deciding cases according to their own policy preferences rather than by applying the law impartially according to its original public meaning. They have become enamored of ideas like "living constitutionalism," the theory that the Constitution evolves and changes not through the amendment process set out in the Constitution itself, but as a result of the decisions of judges who supposedly serve as the supreme social arbiters. They have drawn on external sources like foreign laws when the outcome they desired did not comport with the original public meaning of the law under review.

> The danger is not, that the judges will be too firm in resisting public opinion … but, that they will be ready to yield themselves to the passions, and politics, and prejudices of the day.
>
> —Joseph Story, 1833

Liberal activist Justice William Brennan famously said that "With five votes you can do anything around here"—five votes being a majority of the Supreme Court. Living up to Brennan's boast, the federal courts have awarded the federal government power to regulate matters well beyond its constitutional authority. The courts themselves have taken over school systems and prisons for decades at a time, created new rights found nowhere in the Constitution, whittled away at constitutional rights (like property rights) that they apparently dislike, and asserted that they have the authority to decide questions concerning how to conduct the War on Terror that are constitutionally reserved to Congress and the President.

The courts have increasingly intervened on what are properly political questions. They have thereby undermined the ability of the American people to decide important issues through their elected representatives. Not surprisingly, the courts have become increasingly politicized institutions, and the nomination and confirmation of judges has also been politicized.

The Constitution is resilient, and it provides its own mechanism for renewal. The President nominates, and the Senate confirms, federal judges to serve during good behavior. If America is to be again a country of laws, and not of men, the people must demand that their President nominate and Senators confirm only judges who will conform to the proper role of a judge, and rule based upon the words and the original public meaning of the Constitution.

> *"Neither liberals nor conservatives want judges taking government officials' factual assertions at face value and failing to identify and evaluate the government's true ends when the Constitution is actually implicated—nor should they."*

Justices Should Determine the Motives of Government When Making Rulings

Evan Bernick

In the following viewpoint, Evan Bernick proposes an approach he calls "judicial engagement" as an alternative to "judicial restraint." This approach, argues Bernick, would require justices to engage in impartial efforts to determine if the government's actions are constitutionally proper. This viewpoint was written shortly after the death of Justice Antonin Scalia and President Obama's subsequent nomination of the moderate judge Merrick Garland to replace him. Garland's nomination brought to the fore arguments about judicial interpretation. Bernick is a legal scholar and assistant director at the Institute of Justice.

"The Supreme Court Needs a New Judicial Approach: The Case for Judicial Engagement," by Evan Bernick, Cato Institute, September 12, 2016. https://www.cato-unbound. org/2016/09/12/evan-bernick/supreme-court-needs-new-judicial-approach-case-judicial-engagement. Reprinted by permission.

As you read, consider the following questions:

1. What approach does Bernick believe the Supreme Court justices should be committed to?
2. How does Bernick define "individual rights"?
3. What is "Chevron deference"?

As goes the Supreme Court, so goes the trajectory of American constitutional law—and partisans on both sides of the political aisle know it. It is therefore entirely unsurprising that the passing of Justice Antonin Scalia and President Barack Obama's subsequent nomination of Judge Merrick Garland to the Court have given rise to a heated political conflict and produced no end of commentary and strategic advice from scholars and pundits.

But there has been little discussion of precisely what kind of approach Justice Scalia's eventual replacement should take in constitutional cases. We hear of particular decisions that must either be preserved or overruled but virtually nothing about how the next Justice should evaluate assertions of government power. The silence concerning the latter subject is striking. The outcomes of many constitutional cases turn upon whether judges carefully scrutinize the evidence in the record, strive to identify the government's true ends, and evaluate the constitutional propriety of those ends, or instead systematically defer to the government officials' factual assertions and assurances that they are pursuing proper ends.

In this essay, I will argue that all Americans who believe that it is the function of the federal judiciary to "guard the Constitution and the rights of individuals" should insist that the next Justice be committed to a particular judicial approach. That approach is judicial engagement.

I will begin by identifying a constitutional duty that any proposed judicial approach must equip judges to discharge: the duty of independent judgment. I will go on to discuss historical attacks on independent judgment and corresponding calls for "judicial restraint," understood as systematic judicial deference to the legislative and executive branches in constitutional cases, and detail how judicial restraint has failed to deliver constitutionally limited government. Finally, I will explain how judicial engagement can ensure that Americans receive the kind of adjudication that they expect and deserve in our courts of law.

"The Duty of the Power": The Constitutional Duty of Independent Judgment

Article III's textual commands to judges are sparse. The Constitution assumes that judges will bring an understanding of their constitutional duties to their office. "The judicial power" incorporates a rich conception of judicial duty that can be traced back through hundreds of years of Anglo-American jurisprudence.

As Professor Philip Hamburger has shown in his exhaustive historical study, Law and Judicial Duty, common law judges were understood to have a duty of independent judgment—a duty to independently interpret and give effect to what Chief Justice Edward Coke called the "artificial reason" of the law of the land. Judges were not to give way to external or internal will—that is, to beliefs or desires of government officials, or to judges' own beliefs and desires that had no foundation in the law. In eighteenth-century America, this ideal of independent judgment had profoundly countermajoritarian implications. The principal threats to liberty during the founding era came from state legislatures and popular majorities that (as Hamburger puts it) "repeatedly threatened the freedom of various racial, religious, political, and propertied minorities."

The establishment of a structurally independent federal judiciary, staffed by judges who were duty-bound to give effect to "[t]his Constitution" was not, as one scholar recently put it, a mere "afterthought." When the Supreme Court in *Marbury* v. *Madison* (1803) declared the Judiciary Act of 1789 to be void, it was discharging a well-established duty of independent judgment. That duty is central to maintaining the rule of law that the Constitution is designed to establish and safeguarding individual rights that it is designed to secure.

The Progressive Assault on Independent Judgment and the Rise of Judicial Restraint

In the late nineteenth century, Harvard Professor James Bradley Thayer and a small collection of students initiated a vigorous attack on the ideal of independent judgment. These students would go on to become some of the most influential jurists and scholars in the nation's history, including Oliver Wendell Holmes, Jr., Louis Brandeis, Learned Hand, and Alexander Bickel.

Thayer viewed the Constitution as pervasively indeterminate and constitutional law as largely the product of judges' beliefs and desires—their will. As Hand would recount, Thayer taught that "most of constitutional law had been constructed out of circular propositions, which justified the predetermined attitudes of the judges." What, then, should judges do? In an influential 1893 article, Thayer argued that judges should broadly defer to majoritarian will—that they should only strike down congressional statutes if their unconstitutionality is "so clear that it is not open to rational question."

Such judicial restraint was attractive to progressives, who rejected the very concepts of limited government and individual rights as outmoded, and who had come to perceive the judiciary as an impediment to social and economic goals that they hoped to achieve through majoritarian politics. In his important book *Rehabilitating Lochner*, Professor David E. Bernstein documents how the Supreme Court of the late nineteenth and early twentieth century was far more deferential to economic regulations than conventional wisdom has long held. But the Court did make genuine efforts to determine whether regulations that burdened individual rights were actually designed to protect public health and safety, or served only to impose the mere will of the politically powerful. Such rights included the right to earn a living in the lawful occupation of one's choice—a right that the Court (properly) deemed to be protected by the Fourteenth Amendment.

Lochner v. *New York* (1905) showcased the then-prevailing legal order and the critique that brought about the fall of that order. In *Lochner*, the Court held that a provision of New York's Bakeshop Act that prohibited the employment of biscuit, cake, and bread bakers for more than ten hours in one day or sixty hours in one week arbitrarily deprived bakers and their employers of their "liberty of contract as well as of person." Writing for the Court, Justice Rufus Peckham determined that there was "no reasonable foundation for holding [the hours provision] to be necessary or appropriate as a health law" and concluded that it was "in reality, passed from other motives."

But it is Justice Oliver Wendell Holmes' pithy, pungent dissent that everyone remembers. Holmes denied that the principle of "liberty of contract as well as of person" was embodied in the Constitution or even consistently enforced in the Court's jurisprudence. He put forward an alternative principle: "[T]he word liberty in the Fourteenth Amendment is perverted when it is held to prevent the natural outcome of a dominant opinion, unless it can be said that a rational and fair man necessarily would admit that the statute proposed would infringe fundamental principles." Thus did a version of Thayer's "clear-error" rule make its way into the United States Reports.

Holmes' dissent, widely celebrated by progressives, was the future. Eventually, the Court would adopt a posture of systematic judicial restraint in all cases involving "economic" regulations. A majority of justices came to believe that Holmes had been right about the Court's jurisprudence. The Court did, however, carve out some ground on which to stand in the future. In a famous footnote (known today simply as "Footnote Four") in the 1938 case of *United States* v. *Carolene Products*, the Court laid the foundation for what would become a defining feature of our jurisprudence—the framework of "tiered scrutiny," according to which different standards of review are deployed in different constitutional contexts.

While economic regulations would be presumed constitutional until proven otherwise, Footnote Four left open the possibility that legislation implicating rights that were specifically enumerated in the Bill of Rights, targeting "discrete or insular minorities," or interfering with the political process might receive "more exacting judicial scrutiny" (today, "heightened scrutiny," which requires the government to affirmatively demonstrate the constitutionality of its actions.)

The Warren Court: The Decline of Progressive Judicial Restraint and the Rise of Conservative Judicial Restraint

As Footnote Four suggested, progressives' commitment to judicial restraint did not last. The political and jurisprudential career of Earl Warren, appointed Chief Justice of the Supreme Court in 1953, is illustrative. Warren's jurisprudence was informed by his prior experience as an executive official in California, which taught him that progressives' vision of (in the words of G. Edward White's illuminating biography) "a beneficent government, staffed by nonpartisan experts" needed to be amended. Warren saw firsthand how much room there was for government officials to abuse their power, and his battles with the California legislature led him to become "a thoroughgoing skeptic about the representativeness or democratic character of the legislative forum."

The cases with which Chief Justice Warren was soon confronted would confirm his experience and lead him to adopt a judicial approach that progressives once rejected. No case did more to forge Warren's approach than *Brown* v. *Board of Education* (1954), in which the Court unanimously held racial segregation in public education to be unconstitutional. White explains that Brown led Warren to bring about a "return to a scrutinizing role for the courts that was of longer standing in American life than the role that Holmes helped to originate." The Warren Court's most famous cases primarily saw the Court carefully scrutinizing and invalidating assertions of government power. Many of these cases fell outside of the Footnote Four framework—among them, cases involving unenumerated "fundamental" rights like the right to marry, the right of married couples to use contraceptives, and the right to associate with others for lawful purposes.

The modern conservative legal movement was borne of opposition to the Warren Court's jurisprudence. Conservatives charged that many of Court's decisions were the product of the justices' mere will rather than law. They adopted Holmes' critique of the Lochner Court, and turned it against the Warren Court's "judicial activism."

Conservative restraint proponents did not attack the ideal of independent judgment free from will—they argued that the Warren Court was disregarding that ideal. But their proposed judicial approach differed scarcely, if at all, from that of the progressives. The Constitution, they contended, did not protect any unenumerated rights—thus, neither the right of married couples to use contraceptives nor the right to earn a living merited judicial enforcement. As Judge Robert Bork memorably put it, "in wide areas of life majorities are entitled to rule if they wish, simply because they are majorities" (emphasis added)—and outside of a few settings, judges who required government officials to offer more than majoritarian will to justify legislation were anathema.

Judicial Restraint in Practice: The Decline of the Rule of Law

Calls for judicial restraint have demonstrably failed to produce constitutionally constrained government. By requiring judges to abdicate their duty of independent judgment, judicial restraint prevents the judiciary from maintaining the rule of law.

For every governmental depredation of which conservatives rightly complain, one can point to a doctrine that tips the judicial scales in the direction of government officials' mere will. Consider "Chevron deference," which requires judges to defer to federal executive agencies' interpretations of congressional statutes when agency officials write and enforce regulations pursuant to the

Judicial Restraint

Judicial restraint has a long history in American legal theory and case law. US Supreme Court decisions as early as *Fletcher* v. *Peck* (1810) state that judges should strike down laws only if they "feel a clear and strong conviction" of unconstitutionality. Early scholars also endorsed the idea; one notable example is Harvard law professor James Bradley Thayer (1831–1902), who observed that a legislator might vote against a law because he believed it unconstitutional but nonetheless, if he later became a judge, properly vote to uphold it on the grounds of restraint.

The general effect of judicial restraint is to allow the legislature and executive greater freedom to formulate policy. Its political valence has thus varied depending on the relative positions of the Supreme Court and the elected branches. In the first half of the 20th century, judicial restraint was generally invoked by liberals in the hopes of preventing courts from striking down Progressive and New Deal economic regulation. Supreme Court justices associated with progressive restraint include Oliver Wendell Holmes, Jr. (served 1902–32), Louis Brandeis (1916–39), and Felix Frankfurter (1939–62).

In the second half of the century, during the tenure of Chief Justice Earl Warren (1953–69), the Supreme Court began taking positions more liberal than the states and the federal government, and restraint became a common conservative political theme. Justices endorsing restraint during this period included John Marshall Harlan (1955–71) and Frankfurter, who continued to endorse the principle even as its politics shifted around him.

As with its political valence, judicial restraint does not have a consistent normative value. In general, restraint is typically considered desirable on the grounds that in a democracy elected officials should play the primary role in making policy. Courts that are insufficiently deferential to elected legislators and executives may usurp that role and unduly constrain democratic self-governance. On the other hand, protection of constitutional rights, particularly those of minorities, demands a certain degree of judicial assertiveness. A restrained court may decline to interfere with serious infringements on such rights, and indeed some of the Supreme Court's most reviled decisions—including *Plessy* v. *Ferguson* (1896), in which the court upheld racial segregation of railroad cars and established the "separate-but-equal" doctrine, and *Korematsu* v. *United States* (1944), in which the court upheld race-based discrimination against Japanese Americans during World War II—fit this pattern.

"Judicial Restraint," by Kermit Roosevelt, Encylopedia Britannica. Inc.

statutes unless those interpretations are "unreasonable." There is also "Auer deference," a doctrine which commands sweeping judicial deference to agencies' interpretations of regulations that they write and enforce. Consider also the modern rational basis test, the standard of review that is used to evaluate all government burdens that do not implicate one of a handful of rights that the Supreme Court has deemed "fundamental." In *FCC v. Beach Communications* (1993), the Court stated that challengers in rational basis cases must "negative every conceivable basis which might support [the government's actions]"—a logically impossible feat. Rational basis review has led the Supreme Court and lower courts to uphold patently protectionist restrictions on everything from pushcart food vending to floristry to teeth-whitening. It even led the Court to approve the bulldozing of an entire working-class neighborhood by a private corporation, exercising the government's power of eminent domain, for so-called "economic development" in the infamous case of *Kelo v. New London* (2005).

Few decisions illustrate judicial restraint's failure to restrain government as vividly as did *NFIB v. Sebelius*, the 2012 decision in which the Court upheld the Affordable Care Act's individual mandate to purchase government-approved health insurance. Chief Justice John Roberts cast the deciding vote and wrote the opinion for a fractured Court, determining that the individual mandate was definitely not authorized by the Commerce Clause but could be construed as a tax authorized by Congress' taxing power—even though the mandate is referred to some 18 times as a "penalty" in the text of the ACA. Roberts' reasoning was the product of his commitment to restraint—he understood himself to be obliged to adopt any "fairly possible" interpretation that would "save [the statute] from unconstitutionality." Judicial restraint thus facilitated the greatest expansion of federal power since the New Deal.

Liberals too have reason to reject judicial restraint. All of the concerns about majoritarian politics that led the Warren Court to reject restraint still apply today. Further, a growing body of public choice scholarship has shown that legislation does not even reliably embody majoritarian preferences—it often embodies only the preferences of politically powerful special interests. Finally, majoritarian politics cannot protect criminal defendants or victims of injuries by law enforcement officers. For the latter, judicial deference is a recipe for rights-violations without effective recourse. Consider the impact of the Court-fashioned doctrine of qualified immunity, which insulates government officials from civil liability for constitutional and statutory violations unless their actions violate "clearly established" law. Qualified immunity has become an almost insuperable bar to civil liability for all but the most egregious and incompetent official misconduct. The result: a status quo of constitutional rights without remedies.

Judicial Engagement: A Call to Judicial Duty

Few have discussed in any great detail what the next Justice should do. But what judges are doing in a number of important areas of law is profoundly troubling. The next Justice will be in a position to either ensure that we have more of the same or to challenge the status quo and point the way towards a different approach.

The judicial approach that I advocate is called judicial engagement. As defined and defended by my colleague at the Institute for Justice, constitutional litigator Clark Neily, in his book *Terms of Engagement*, judicial engagement consists of a genuinely impartial effort to assess the constitutional propriety of the government's true ends and means in light of evidence in the record. It provides that the government must bear the burden of producing evidence and must articulate a reason for its actions when those actions are challenged in court. Judges must determine whether the government's actions are in fact calculated to achieve a constitutionally proper end of government.

The text of the Constitution does not command any particular degree of judicial deference. Judicial engagement is a constitutional construction that does not contradict the text and is consistent with a central function (at common law and in the early American republic, the "spirit") of Article III—ensuring that those burdened by governmental actions that they believe to be unlawful have access to a neutral forum in which government power is measured against the law of the land. Judicial engagement treats both parties as presumptive equals, recognizes that one party is seeking to impose its will upon the other, and requires the party seeking to impose its will upon the other to offer evidence and a reason that justifies its actions. Any deference to mere will would require a departure from the duty of independent judgment—judicial engagement ensures, to the extent possible, that mere will does not sway judgment.

We know that such engagement is possible. Engagement takes place routinely in cases in which judges apply heightened scrutiny, whether intermediate or strict. We occasionally find the hallmarks of engagement even in cases in which the Court has said that it is applying the rational basis test. For example, in *City of Cleburne* v. *Cleburne Living Center* (1985), the Court held to be irrational and therefore unconstitutional a decision by a city government to deny a permit for a group home for the mentally disabled. The Court in Cleburne independently evaluated the evidence and rejected asserted purposes that were implausible in light of that evidence, ultimately finding that only "irrational prejudice" could explain the decision. (For example, the Court found the asserted purpose of "avoiding concentration of population and… lessening congestion of the streets" to be implausible because "apartment houses, fraternity and sorority houses, hospitals and the like, [could] freely locate in the area without a permit.")

The questions of what rights are protected by the Constitution and what reasons are constitutionally proper are hotly contested. But there is substantial agreement that genuine constitutional rights should be enforced, and that judges should distinguish constitutionally proper from constitutionally improper reasons for burdening people's rights or treating them differently. Liberals have celebrated recent decisions in which the Supreme Court and lower courts have invalidated regulations of abortion clinics and voter-ID laws, precisely because they believe that judges in those cases engaged in fact-sensitive review and careful means-ends analysis. Conservatives have criticized the Supreme Court for declining to review a Ninth Circuit Court of Appeals decision upholding Washington state regulations that require pharmacists and pharmacies to dispense emergency contraceptives, precisely because they believe that the court below brushed aside evidence that the state deliberately singled out religious conduct. Neither liberals nor conservatives want judges taking government officials' factual assertions at face value and failing to identify and evaluate the government's true ends when the Constitution is actually implicated—nor should they.

Defending Reason's Republic

The partisanship that has dominated the debate over Justice Scalia's replacement has been dispiriting if predictable. But we must not allow that partisanship to obscure a fundamental question that has yet to be sufficiently explored: How should the next Justice adjudicate? Article III promises a means through which ordinary Americans can put government power to the test of the principles of reason in our law. To the extent that Americans who stand to lose their liberty, their property, their livelihoods, or even their lives are denied adjudication that is driven by independent judgment rather than will, they do not live under a government of laws but of men—and their rights are insecure. For the sake of the rule of law, the next Justice must be prepared to engage.

> *"[Judicial restraint] calls on unelected judges to recognize their proper role in a democracy, making sure that when they foist their will on over 300 million Americans, the exercise of that power is clearly authorized by the Constitution and the rule of law."*

Judicial Restraint Is Not an Abdication of the Responsibility to Challenge the Will of the Minority

Barry P. McDonald

In the following viewpoint, Barry P. McDonald takes issue with Evan Bernick's argument in the previous viewpoint, that judges should examine the rationale or need for laws they are reviewing. McDonald defends a particular approach to judicial restraint and argues that Bernick is troubled by the Court's approach and urges "heightened scrutiny" of the need for the questioned law in only certain types of cases. Barry P. McDonald is a professor of law at Pepperdine University in Malibu, California.

"The Case for Judicial Disengagement… Except Where Appropriate," by Barry P. McDonald, Cato Institute, September 19, 2016. https://www.cato-unbound. org/2016/09/19/barry-p-mcdonald/case-judicial-disengagement-except-where- appropriate. Reprinted by permission.

As you read, consider the following questions:

1. What valuable lesson does the author believe can be learned from the Lochner era?

2. What, according to this author, is the "essence of the rule of law"?

3. What is McDonald's biggest complaint about Bernick's argument?

The day is gone when this Court uses the Due Process Clause … to strike down state laws, regulatory of business and industrial conditions, because they may be unwise, improvident, or out of harmony with a particular school of thought. … For protection against abuses by legislatures the people must resort to the polls, not to the courts." So wrote Justice William O. Douglas for a unanimous Court in 1955 after that body had learned a valuable lesson from the Lochner era—in a democracy, it is not for five or more unelected judges to second guess the economic policy decisions of the people's elected representatives. Yet Evan Bernick urges a return to the Lochner approach of judges vigorously scrutinizing the importance or need for laws adopted by those representatives whenever they are alleged to conflict with any "genuine constitutional right." And he does so under a new veneer: the duty of judges to exercise independent judgment or "judicially engage," an approach he equates with the judicial practice of applying heightened scrutiny to challenged laws in certain areas of constitutional law.

This argument has many problems, most notably the implication that exercising independent judgment is the same thing as applying such scrutiny. It is not. I am all for Supreme Court justices and other judges applying "principles of reason in our law," as Bernick puts it. In other words, judges should and do have a duty to apply legal rules in a neutral, objective and principled fashion when deciding cases—as much as possible keeping their own political and ideological preferences, and those of political majorities, out of the mix when doing so. This is the essence of the rule of law, and not the rule of particular individuals wearing black robes or that of transient majorities.

Moreover, judges should adhere to this practice no matter what degree of scrutiny they apply to a challenged law—be it strict or vigorous scrutiny (where the government bears a very heavy burden of showing constitutionality), intermediate scrutiny or a general balancing of interests (where the government bears a more realistic chance of demonstrating constitutionality), or the deferential scrutiny that Bernick complains of where the plaintiff bears a heavy burden of demonstrating the unconstitutionality of a law. The level of scrutiny the Court applies is an analytical tool based on its judgment about the importance of the right allegedly being infringed or the suspectness of the government's actions in passing a law. Independent judgment, on the other hand, should be a pervasive judicial philosophy and practice no matter what tools a court is applying to aid its review.

What Bernick is really complaining about is which rights the Court has chosen to apply heightened scrutiny to, and those it has judged to be worthy of only minimal judicial review. The former includes those due process rights of personal autonomy deemed fundamental or important, and certain equal protection, free speech and freedom of religion rights where illicit government discrimination seems to be afoot. Notably absent from this list, however, are the conservative favorites of economic and property rights. After the Lochner era, the Court decided that protection for the latter sort of rights was best left to the push and tug of the political process rather than the judiciary. As noted, this decision was based on the notion that heightened judicial protection for such rights inevitably involved courts in the business of making judgments about economic and social policy that they were ill-equipped to make—and that were more appropriate for legislatures to make in a democratic republic.

Now one can certainly make a decent argument that the Court overreacted to the Lochner era criticisms, and that economic and property rights do not deserve the severity of downgraded constitutional treatment they have been given—particularly in cases where it seems that special interest groups have captured the legislature or government bureaucrats are pursuing agendas divorced from the popular will. But the product of such an argument should be a discussion about the importance of those rights and the ability of courts to protect them consistent with democratic principles, rather than an end run around that discussion by urging heightened scrutiny for all rights—and thereby elevating the treatment of economic and property rights through the back door.

Which brings me to my biggest complaint about Bernick's arguments concerning independent judgment. Not only are they misguided in equating such judgment with a given level of judicial scrutiny, but they miss the boat in terms of where independent judgment is really needed. As noted, the level of scrutiny used in a particular case is a function of the Court's a priori determination about whether to recognize an asserted right and how much importance to accord it. That is where most of the judicial work is done in a particular case, since the particular scrutiny applied too often tends to be a post hoc rationale for a result driven by the initial "ranking" (e.g., should an asserted due process right be deemed fundamental or not, or should a non-discrimination claim be viewed as implicating a suspect class). If the right is ranked as really important or the government's action suspect, strict scrutiny applies and the law will be invalidated; if not, the dreaded rational basis review applies and the law will be upheld (unless some sort of middle tier scrutiny is used). And it is that initial determination that generates the criticism that Supreme Court justices are either making up rights that cannot fairly be derived from the Constitution, or they are otherwise according rights importance (or not) depending upon their personal ideological preferences.

Examples of such contested rights abound. Rights to gay marriage, abortion, and even the Lochnerian liberty of contract that Bernick applauds, have all been inferred from a constitutional provision that protects people from being deprived of "liberty" without due process of law—a provision designed to ensure the government uses fair and lawful procedures when denying someone their liberty, and not affirmative rights against a government that complies with them. A right to keep guns in one's home (and perhaps other places) for purposes of general self-defense has been found in a provision that was designed to prevent the professional standing army created by the new Constitution from disarming the citizen-soldier militias of the states—just in case that army was used to oppress Americans. A right of large corporations to spend their earnings to get favored politicians elected has been found in free speech guarantees designed to ensure Americans would be able to freely debate and keep tabs on what the new federal government they were creating was doing. To make matters worse, virtually all of these rights were found to exist, and to deserve the heightened scrutiny Bernick extols, by bare majorities of five justices coalescing in predictable ideological voting blocs. And this problem of "politics dressed up as law" is not limited to the enforcement of constitutional rights. As the Obamacare decision illustrates, it also extends to questions about the nature and scope of federal power. There, the key ruling depriving Congress Commerce Clause power to pass the law was decided along typical ideological voting lines, even though Chief Justice Roberts joined the liberal wing of the Court to find Taxing Clause power for the law, which he probably did to avoid even harsher criticisms of a politicized Court.

This state of affairs is the exact opposite of one might expect from a Court that was truly exercising "independent judgment" grounded in neutral legal principles. If one wants to urge Supreme Court justices to exercise more of such judgment, this is the place where one should make a stand—particularly when the advocate admits the question of what rights the Constitution protects is "hotly contested." To urge greater judicial engagement and independent judgment to protect "genuine constitutional rights" is simply ignoring the huge elephant in the room. Bernick also argues that such greater engagement is needed to prevent majorities from trampling individual rights. But when the very existence and strength of rights involve such debatable and contestable judgments that are being made in the manner described above, who do you want recognizing and protecting them in a self-governing democracy? Five lawyers appointed to the Court who do not even reflect the diversity of values and beliefs of Americans generally— almost all being drawn from the Boston to Washington, DC corridor—or Americans themselves? The answer seems obvious.

Accordingly, I would not attack judicial restraint as the abdication of a judge's role to vigorously challenge the will of the majority whenever an individual right is alleged to be implicated. Properly understood, such restraint should be praised. It calls on unelected judges to recognize their proper role in a democracy, making sure that when they foist their will on over 300 million Americans, the exercise of that power is clearly authorized by the Constitution and the rule of law. If it is not, if claims of constitutional right are open to honest debate by fair and reasonable people, deference to majoritarian resolutions of those issues in the give and take of the political process is the most appropriate course. At least that is the judicial attitude I hope to see in our next Supreme Court justice.

> "*The due process article is a restraint on the legislative as well as on the executive and judicial powers of the government.*"

The Particulars of Due Process Are Still Being Debated

New World Encyclopedia

The concept behind the Bill of Rights actually began in England in the thirteenth century, with the Magna Carta, a document that limited the powers of the king over the citizens without "due process of law." That doctrine became part of "the law of the land," which meant that the king had to obey it just like everyone else. In the following viewpoint, you will learn how that concept has come to be a part of the US law, and how over the years, the implementation of due process has been debated in matters that come under judicial review.

As you read, consider the following questions:

1. What was the only state to request the addition of "due process" language in the Constitution?
2. What did "due process" come to mean in the United States and why was the Fourteenth Amendment necessary?
3. How do you think that the "due process" clause protects individual privacy?

I n the early United States, the terms law of the land and due process were used somewhat interchangeably. The 1776 Constitution of Maryland, for example, used the language of Magna Carta, including the law of the land phrase. In New York, a statutory bill of rights was enacted in 1787, and it contained four different due process clauses.

New York was the only state that asked Congress to add "due process" language to the US Constitution. New York ratified the US Constitution and proposed the following amendment in 1788: "[N]o Person ought to be taken imprisoned or disseised of his freehold, or be exiled or deprived of his Privileges, Franchises, Life, Liberty or Property but by due process of Law."

In response to this proposal from New York, James Madison drafted a Due Process Clause for Congress. Madison cut out some language, and inserted the word without, which had not been proposed by New York. Congress then adopted the exact wording that Madison proposed, after Madison explained that the Due Process Clause would not be sufficient to protect various other rights:

> Although I know whenever the great rights, the trial by jury, freedom of the press, or liberty of conscience, come in question in that body [Parliament], the invasion of them is resisted by able advocates, yet their Magna Charta does not contain any one provision for the security of those rights, respecting which the people of America are most alarmed.

No state or federal constitution in the United States had ever before utilized any "due process" wording, prior to 1791 when the federal Bill of Rights was ratified. However, when the US Constitution took effect in 1789, it did contain a Supremacy Clause, which specified that the Constitution itself, and federal statutes enacted pursuant to the Constitution, would be the supreme "law of the land." As mentioned, in the early United States, the terms law of the land and due process were used somewhat interchangeably.

By the middle of the nineteenth century, "due process of law" was interpreted by the US Supreme Court to mean that "it was not left to the legislative power to enact any process which might be devised. The due process article is a restraint on the legislative as well as on the executive and judicial powers of the government, and cannot be so construed as to leave Congress free to make any process 'due process of law' by its mere will." But determining what those restraints are has been a subject of considerable disagreement.

Procedural Due Process Basics

In the United States, criminal prosecutions and civil cases are governed by explicit guarantees of procedural rights under the Bill of Rights, most of which have been incorporated under the Fourteenth Amendment to the States. Due process has also been construed to generally protect the individual so that statutes, regulations, and enforcement actions must ensure that no one is deprived of "life, liberty, or property" without a fair opportunity to affect the judgment or result. ... In 1934, the United States Supreme Court held that due process is violated "if a practice or rule offends some principle of justice so rooted in the traditions and conscience of our people as to be ranked as fundamental."

Modern substantive due process doctrine protects rights such as the right to privacy, under which rights of private sexual activity (*Lawrence* v. *Texas*), contraception (*Griswold* v. *Connecticut*), and abortion (*Roe* v. *Wade*) fall, as well as most of the substantive protections of the Bill of Rights. However, what are seen as failures to protect enough of our basic liberties, and what are seen as past abuses and present excesses of this doctrine, continue to spur debate over its use.

Judicial Review of Substantive Due Process Violations

When a law or other act of government is challenged as a violation of individual liberty under the Due Process Clause, courts nowadays primarily use two forms of scrutiny, or judicial review. This inquiry balances the importance of the governmental interest being served and the appropriateness of the government's method of implementation against the resulting infringement of individual rights. If the governmental action infringes upon a fundamental right, the highest level of review—strict scrutiny—is used. In order to pass strict scrutiny review, the law or act must be narrowly tailored to a compelling government interest.

When the governmental restriction restricts liberty in a manner that does not implicate a fundamental right, rational basis review is used. Here a legitimate government interest is enough to pass this review. This means that the government's goal must simply be something that it is acceptable for the government to pursue. The means used by the legislation only have to be reasonable for getting to the government's goals; they need not be the best. Under a rational basis test, the burden of proof is on the challenger. Thus, it is rare that laws are overturned after a rational basis test, although this is not unheard of.

There is also a middle level of scrutiny, called intermediate scrutiny, but it is primarily used in Equal Protection cases rather than in Due Process cases: "The standards of intermediate scrutiny have yet to make an appearance in a due process case."

Incorporation of the Bill of Rights into Due Process

Incorporation is the legal doctrine by which the Bill of Rights, either in full or in part, is applied to the states through the Fourteenth Amendment's Due Process Clause. Incorporation started in 1897 with a takings case, continued with *Gitlow* v. *New York* (1925) which was a First Amendment case, and accelerated in the 1940s and 1950s. Justice Hugo Black famously favored the jot-for-jot incorporation of the entire Bill of Rights. Justice Felix Frankfurter, however—joined later by Justice John M. Harlan—felt that the federal courts should only apply those sections of the Bill of Rights whose abridgment would deny a "fundamental right." It was the latter course that the Warren Court of the 1960s took, although, almost all of the Bill of Rights has now been incorporated jot-for-jot against the states.

The basis for incorporation is substantive due process regarding enumerated substantive rights, and procedural due process regarding enumerated procedural rights. The role of the incorporation doctrine in applying the guarantees of the Bill of Rights to the states is just as notable as the use of due process to define new fundamental rights that are not explicitly guaranteed by the Constitution's text. In both cases, the question has been whether the right asserted is "fundamental," so that, just as not all proposed "new" constitutional rights are afforded judicial recognition, not all provisions of the Bill of Rights have been deemed sufficiently fundamental to warrant enforcement against the states.

Some people, such as Justice Black, have argued that the Privileges or Immunities Clause of the Fourteenth Amendment would be a more appropriate textual source for the incorporation doctrine. The Court has not taken that course, and some point to the treatment given to the Privileges or Immunities Clause in the 1873 Slaughterhouse Cases as a reason why. Although, the Slaughterhouse Court did not expressly preclude application of the Bill of Rights to the states, the Clause largely ceased to be invoked in opinions of the Court following the Slaughterhouse Cases, and when incorporation did begin, it was under the rubric of due process. Scholars who share Justice Black's view, such as Akhil Amar, argue that the Framers of the Fourteenth Amendment, like Senator Jacob Howard and Congressman John Bingham, included a Due Process Clause in the Fourteenth Amendment for the following reason: "By incorporating the rights of the Fifth Amendment, the privileges or immunities clause would…have prevented states from depriving 'citizens' of due process. Bingham, Howard, and company wanted to go even further by extending the benefits of state due process to aliens."

The Supreme Court has consistently held that Fifth Amendment due process means substantially the same as Fourteenth Amendment due process, and therefore the original meaning of the former is relevant to the incorporation doctrine of the latter. When the Bill of Rights was originally proposed by Congress in 1789 to the states, various substantive and procedural rights were "classed according to their affinity to each other" instead of being submitted to the states "as a single act to be adopted or rejected in the gross," as James Madison put it. Roger Sherman explained in 1789 that each amendment "may be passed upon distinctly by the States, and any one that is adopted by three fourths of the legislatures may become a part of the Constitution." Thus, the states were allowed to reject the Sixth Amendment, for example, while ratifying all of the other amendments including the Due Process Clause; in that case, the rights in the Sixth Amendment would not have been incorporated against the federal government. The doctrine of incorporating the content of other amendments into "due process" was thus an innovation, when it began in 1925 with the Gitlow case, and this doctrine remains controversial today.

Periodical and Internet Sources Bibliography

The following articles have been selected to supplement the diverse views presented in this chapter.

Ashley Baker, "The Supreme Court Should Exercise Judicial in the Microsoft Data Case," *The Hill*, October 22, 2017. http://thehill.com/opinion/technology/356621-the-supreme court-should-exercise-judicial-restraint-in-microsoft-data.

David Davenport, "Is Gay Marriage the Product of Judicial Activism?" *Forbes*, July 2, 2013. https://www.forbes.com/sites/ daviddavenport/2013/07/02/is-gay-marriage-the-product -of-judicial-activism/#5532b7623642.

Jill Lepore, "The History Test: How Should the Courts Use History?" *New Yorker*, March 27, 2017. https://www.newyorker.com/ magazine/2017/03/27/weaponizing-the-past.

Geoffrey R. Stone, "Our Fill in the Blank Constitution," *New York Times*, April 13, 2010. http://www.nytimes.com/2010/04/14/ opinion/14stone.html?mtrref=www.google.com&gwh= 819654516D3AF40D1D5D5222386BA16B&gwt=pay&asset- Type=opinion.

Jeffrey Toobin, "The Conservative Pipeline to the Supreme Court," *New Yorker*, April 17, 2017. https://www.newyorker.com/ magazine/2017/04/17/the-conservative-pipeline-to-the -supreme-court.

Edward Whelan, "Rand Paul Is Wrong: Judicial Restraint Is Right," *National Review*, January 15, 2015. http://www.nationalreview .com/article/396480/rand-paul-wrong-judicial-restraint-right -ed-whelan.

Adam J. White, "'We the People' and Constitutional Liberty," *Weekly Standard*, July 11, 2016. http://www.weeklystandard.com/ we-the-people-and-constitutional-liberty/article/2003234.

George F. Will, "Judicial Activism Isn't a Bad Thing," *Washington Post*, January 22, 2014. https://www.washingtonpost.com/opinions/ george-will-judicial-activism-isnt-a-bad-thing/2014/01/22/ 31b41a12-82c7-11e3-8099-9181471f7aaf_story.html?utm_ term=.033ebf50113a.

CHAPTER 4

Has the Court Become Too Political in Interpreting the Bill of Rights?

Chapter Preface

There is a great deal of debate about how much restraint justices should use when deciding whether laws passed by the legislative branch are in keeping with the tenets of the Constitution. In many cases, the opinions people have on these matters aligns roughly, if not exactly, with their political views. Yet the justices themselves are expected to be immune to political considerations. Or at least they used to be. In recent years, politics has come to the bench. There is perhaps no better example of this than the situation after Justice Scalia died in 2016. The Republican-controlled Senate refused to confirm President Obama's choice to replace him (even though that replacement was well-qualified and quite moderate). In fact, many refused to even meet with him. Some legislators announced that they would not confirm an Obama appointment, no matter who was chosen. This was unquestionably a political maneuver.

Yet, as this chapter suggests, justices do not always behave the way the politicians who appoint and confirm them expect them to. Serving on the Supreme Court is a heavy responsibility. Some justices—you will recall some of Justice Antonin Scalia's comments in earlier chapters—occasionally use snark and sarcasm when a more respectful approach might be called for. But in the end, most justices take their mission very seriously, making the decisions that they have determined to be the best reading of the Constitution—even in some cases when that reading is opposed to their own political preferences.

The viewpoints in this chapter examine questions such as whether enforcing rights amounts to political action on the part of the Court, and what consequences result for the nation when that happens.

| "Federalists and Antifederalists could
  not agree on what 'national' meant."

Controversy Is Built In to the Bill of Rights

Jack Lynch

In the following viewpoint, Jack Lynch examines the debate about whether to include a Bill of Rights in the US Constitution. The author explains why the argument against the Bill of Rights was not anti-American or anti-democracy. Though the debate did come down to political positions, the final decision was a matter of balancing ideals and pragmatism. This delicate balance is something that characterizes political discourse in the United States even today. Jack Lynch is a professor of English at Rutgers University; he specializes in the eighteenth century.

As you read, consider the following questions:

1. Madison made several changes in terminology when drafting the Bill of Rights. Why do you think he removed the term "civil rights"?
2. Why, according to some of the arguments at the time, would a bill of rights actually limit, rather than protect, freedoms?
3. According to the viewpoint, what intentions expressed in the Bill of Rights are irreconcilable?

"Debating the Bill of Rights," by Jack Lynch appeared in the Winter 2009 issue of the *Journal of Colonial Williamsburg*. It is reprinted with the permission of The Colonial Williamsburg Foundation.

W hen presidents of the United States want to draw attention to authoritarian regimes elsewhere in the world, they remind us that people suffering under foreign tyrannies enjoy no fundamental rights, no freedom of religion, no freedom of speech, no freedom of assembly. . . . When American secretaries of state want to highlight abusive judicial systems, they note the lack of guarantees of due process, jury trials, and protection against self-incrimination. When lawmakers want to distinguish representative democracy from oppressive police states, they tell stories about unreasonable search and seizure and cruel and unusual punishment. Subjects of unenlightened dictatorships, we are told, lack the rights that make this the land of the free.

What this American set of freedoms has in common is its enshrinement in the Bill of Rights, the first ten amendments to the federal Constitution, ratified in 1791. These principles have not only come to seem as natural as the rights enumerated in the Declaration of Independence; after more than two centuries, they have the authority of Scripture. The ten amendments have almost become the Ten Commandments. Freedom of speech now seems as fundamental as the injunction against murder, and the right to avoid self-incrimination seems as basic to justice as "thou shalt not bear false witness."

It is surprising to discover that these fundamental rights were so nettlesome to the people charged with framing the Constitution. The arguments over the Bill of Rights were sometimes bitter, beginning with whether the federal government should protect individual rights at all. The framers considered opening the Constitution with a list of natural rights, following the lead of most of the state constitutions, but decided against it. The document they sent to the states for ratification in 1787 had little to say on the subject.

That surprised John Adams, then in England, who wrote to Thomas Jefferson, then in Paris, "What think you of a Declaration of Rights? Should not such a Thing have preceded the Model?" Jefferson agreed: he found much to like about the new plan for a federal government, but he objected to "the omission of a bill of rights." He wrote to his fellow Virginian, James Madison, the Constitution's primary author, that "a bill of rights is what the people are entitled to against every government on earth, general or particular, & what no government should refuse, or rest on inference." Events proved that Adams and Jefferson, from across the Atlantic, were more in tune with popular opinion than the members of the Constitutional Convention. Soon people throughout America were clamoring for a list of individual rights, refusing to base their fundamental freedoms on "inference." But nearly as many were vocal in their struggle against any such list.

We cannot assume that those who fought against a bill of rights were reactionary, undemocratic, or anti-American, for some of the fiercest opposition came from the most passionate civil libertarians. Some said a bill of rights would not guarantee but restrict freedoms—that a list of specific rights would imply that they were granted by the government rather than inherent in nature. They also remembered a maxim of common law, expressio unius est exclusio alterius—the mention of one thing amounts to the exclusion of others. Guarantees of freedom of speech, press, religion, and so on might imply that these were the only freedoms to which citizens were entitled. Others said that the federal government could never be in a position to interfere with personal rights—those protections belonged in state constitutions—and that the Constitution should say nothing about them. "Why," asked Alexander Hamilton in "Federalist 84," "declare that things shall not be done which there is no power to do?" After all, the Constitution does not guarantee the right to food or drink, but no one feels the need to protect them from federal interference.

The battle lines were drawn, Federalists on one side and Antifederalists on the other. Federalists called for immediate ratification of the Constitution without amendment, but their united front concealed differences of opinion: some thought a bill of rights an essential first order of business for the new Congress, some believed it unnecessary but harmless, and others thought it an evil to be avoided. The other side was just as divided: some Antifederalists opposed the Constitution only because it lacked a bill of rights, and others opposed it on other grounds and merely used the bill of rights as an excuse to campaign against it.

Madison's change of heart may have tipped the balance in the country at large: he came to agree to "a revisal of the constitution," provided it was "a moderate one." He was, he told Congress on June 8, 1789, "unwilling to see a door opened for a re-consideration of the whole structure of the government," but he took the lead in consulting earlier guarantees of personal freedoms and drafting a set of amendments to the document he had composed two years earlier. The compromise proved effective, winning over enough holdouts to secure a Federalist victory. The states agreed to ratify the Constitution if the first Congress would set to work on a catalog of fundamental rights.

Once it was agreed that there should be a Bill of Rights, there was not universal agreement about which rights should be protected. So familiar and essential are the first ten amendments that many Americans are surprised to discover that Madison originally presented the House of Representatives with a list of seventeen Constitutional revisions, which the Congress whittled down to twelve—and that it was this bill of twelve amendments, not the famous ten, that went to the states for ratification. Two were rejected—one, about apportioning members of the House, has never been ratified; another, about Congressional salaries, was passed as the 27th Amendment in 1992, after 201 years.

The ten that succeeded could provoke controversy. Consider what now stands as the First Amendment, protecting freedom of religion, speech, the press, assembly, and petition. There is nothing more fundamentally American than the freedom of religion, and it seems appropriate that it stands at the head of the list. But what now holds the first position was the fourth amendment as drafted by Madison, and the third as sent to the states for ratification.

June 8, 1789, Madison offered his first draft of a Constitutional amendment to protect religious freedom:

That in article 1st, section 9, between clauses 3 and 4, be inserted these clauses, to wit, The civil rights of none shall be abridged on account of religious belief or worship, nor shall any national religion be established, nor shall the full and equal rights of conscience be in any manner, or on any pretext infringed.

As soon as the amendment was introduced, Congress set to work changing it. Roger Sherman of Connecticut "thought the amendment altogether unnecessary," though most agreed it was needed. The representatives drafting and revising the language were not certain what their words implied. Madison "said, he apprehended the meaning of the words to be, that congress should not establish a religion, and enforce the legal observation of it by law," but Benjamin Huntington of Connecticut "feared . . . that the words might be taken with such latitude as to be extremely hurtful to the cause of religion," since "others might find it convenient to put another construction upon it," disallowing religious observation by the government.

Elbridge Gerry of Massachusetts "Did not like the term national"—Federalists and Antifederalists could not agree on what "national" meant. After listening to the debate, Samuel Livermore of New Hampshire "was not satisfied with that amendment," and on August 15 proposed that it should read, "Congress shall make no laws touching religion, or infringing the rights of conscience." Five days later, Fisher Ames of Massachusetts picked up on Livermore's language and proposed, "Congress shall make no law establishing religion, or to prevent the free exercise thereof, or to infringe the rights of conscience." By the time it left the House, the amendment read, "Congress shall make no law establishing religion or prohibiting the free exercise thereof, nor shall the rights of Conscience be infringed."

September 3, during Senate debate, there came a proposal "to strike out these words, 'Religion or prohibiting the free exercise thereof,' and insert, 'One Religious Sect or Society in preference to others'"—a proposal that had in mind the dangers of sectarianism, though it did not call for officially enforced secularism. The motion failed. The same day there was a motion to omit the article, though the Senate Journal records that it, too, "passed in the Negative." Later in the day the Senate voted down another version: "Congress shall make no law establishing any particular denomination of religion in preference to another, or prohibiting the free exercise thereof, nor shall the rights of conscience be infringed."

The Conference Committee resolved the differences between the House and Senate versions, and proposed, "Congress shall make no Law respecting an establishment of Religion, or prohibiting the free exercise thereof." This is the version that left the Congress on September 25, and was ratified, along with the other rights in the First Amendment, by the states December 15, 1791.

With many scholars urging us to pay attention to the original intent of our Constitution, these drafts are relevant to modern jurisprudence. Most of the differences are small, but all are potentially significant, and over the centuries important Supreme Court of the United States cases have hinged on the smallest matters of expression.

Madison, for example, suggests in his original draft that his main concern is "civil rights," a phrase dropped from the discussion in favor of a guarantee of the "free exercise" of religion. But what can Madison's original intention tell us about how we should interpret the text today? Should "civil rights" be at the heart of our understanding of the amendment, because that is what Madison wanted? Or is it more important that the Congress removed that language in favor of what stands, and therefore specifically rejected that interpretation?

Or, to take another example, a guarantee of "full and equal rights of conscience" appeared in Madison's version; the Senate dropped the language. Does its appearance tell us that freedom of conscience was fundamental to the First Amendment? Does its disappearance tell us that it was unimportant?

Nearly every clause went through the same kinds of revisions, some minute, some sweeping, but all offering new interpretations of the language of the Constitution. In Neil H. Cogan's monumental collection of primary sources, *The Complete Bill of Rights*, the documents of the disputes over the Establishment and Free Exercise clauses fill only the first 82 of the book's 708 pages, suggesting that the Bill of Rights underwent thousands of alterations. Countless modern Constitutional debates—the meaning of "militia" in the Second Amendment, the "right of the people to be secure in their persons" in the Fourth, the definition of "cruel and unusual punishments" in the Eighth—can be illuminated by an examination of the drafts and revisions the texts underwent. That most readers on every side of every question find in these documents what they were looking for should tell us that we have yet to settle the questions of interpretation.

It is important to take the Bill of Rights seriously, but it is wise to remember that its provisions were not engraved in stone. When we talk about recovering the original intent of the Bill of Rights, we have to remember that the document expresses a complicated amalgam of dozens, perhaps hundreds, of intentions, some of which are probably irreconcilable.

Jefferson was convinced that our rights should not merely "rest on inference," and the resulting document did much to clarify the principles we have since come to regard as quintessentially American. But the history of the creation of the Bill of Rights leaves us with many questions, uncertainties, and ambiguities. Perhaps it is only fitting for a nation founded on such a combination of idealistic principles and pragmatic compromise.

*"[FDR's] New Deal firmly established
the government's right to guarantee
a minimum wage for jobholders,
Social Security for elderly Americans,
and targeted subsidies for groups the
president needed for reelection."*

The Right to Economic Security Is Fundamentally Different from the Rights Guaranteed in the Bill of Rights

Burton W. Folsom

Several of the previous viewpoints decry the increased power of the federal government, and the Court's support of that power. In the following viewpoint, Burton W. Folsom tries to determine when Americans became willing to accept this state of affairs. He traces it to what President Franklin Roosevelt called "The Economic Bill of Rights"—namely the assurance that every citizen had the right not only to freedom, but to economic security. Folsom argues that no such right exists, and the idea of providing a measure of economic security is anti-democratic because it requires taxing the rich. Burton Folsom is a professor of history at Hillsdale College and author of FDR Goes to War. *He writes for the Foundation for Economic Education.*

As you read, consider the following questions:

1. Why does this author say the rights outlined by President Roosevelt do not exist? How does he say the right to liberty or to free speech is more natural than the right to a job?

2. Where, according to this author, did FDR get the funds to provide Americans with education and jobs?

3. When you read this article, do you hear any resonances with the current debate over health care?

M any people are perplexed by the new government programs that have changed American life in the last century. So much of this intervention has been damaging, and so much of it is unconstitutional. Can we pinpoint a time, or an event, that led Americans to accept a more powerful central government in their lives?

The intervention has been gradual since the Progressive Era of the early twentieth century, but one event helped crystallize the rising dominance of statist ideas: President Roosevelt's promotion of his Economic Bill of Rights during World War II. FDR announced this new bill of rights during his State of the Union message in January 1944. "Our Economic Bill of Rights," the President said, "like the sacred Bill of Rights of our Constitution itself—must be applied to all citizens." He added, "A new basis of security and prosperity can be established for all—regardless of station, race, or creed." Among others, these new rights included the following:

- the right to a useful and remunerative job in the industries or shops or farms or mines of our nation;
- the right of every family to a decent home;
- the right to a good education;
- the right to adequate medical care and the opportunity to achieve and enjoy good health.

Roosevelt concluded: "All of these rights spell security. And after the war is won we must be prepared to move forward, in the implementation of these rights, to new goals of human happiness and well-being."

Where do Roosevelt's new rights come from? They are not natural rights, or God-given rights, because nature, or God, does not endow man with "a good education," "adequate medical care," or "a decent home." Only if government is the source of rights do Roosevelt's rights have meaning. If an American has a right to "a useful and remunerative job," then government has the obligation to find or provide employment, even if that requires taxing those who have jobs. If an American has a right to "a decent home," whatever size and furnishings that might include, then if necessary, other Americans have the responsibility to pay for that decent home. Thus Roosevelt's new Economic Bill of Rights was revolutionary. To provide these new rights, government would have to tax and redistribute wealth on a massive scale.

The original Bill of Rights was very different. It listed freedoms from government interference, not the freedom to invoke government to fulfill wants. The Founders understood that freedom of speech and religion were natural rights that all people can enjoy without hampering one another's liberty.

During Roosevelt's 12 years in office, he increased government immensely, preparing the nation for the larger government he wanted after the war. His New Deal firmly established the government's right to guarantee a minimum wage for jobholders, Social Security for elderly Americans, and targeted subsidies for groups the president needed for reelection. The Economic Bill of Rights presaged programs for national health care, federal aid to education, and a federal housing authority.

The taxing machinery was also in place. It had to be. Building houses, sending people to college, creating job programs, and providing medical care for many millions of Americans would be costly, and FDR needed a steady torrent of cash to do it all. World War II gave FDR the opportunity to raise taxes and keep them high afterward to support his Economic Bill of Rights.

FDR had increased taxes step by step during his presidency. He started with the rich. In 1932, the year FDR won the presidency, the top marginal tax rate was 25 percent. By 1939, the first year of the European war, FDR had hiked that rate to 79 percent. During World War II he was able to get the rate up to 94 percent on all income over $200,000. The top marginal corporate rate had risen to 90 percent.

Near-Confiscatory Taxes for All

But, as FDR discovered, near-confiscatory taxes on the rich were not enough to pay for the war and not enough to fund houses, education, jobs, and medical care for many millions of Americans after the war. He had to make taxpayers out of most American wage earners. This he achieved by lowering the personal exemption from $1,000 to $500, so only that amount was tax-free. He increased the bottom marginal rate from 4 to 23 percent from 1939 to 1945. Thus when FDR made taxpayers out of most Americans, the revenue from the income tax skyrocketed from just over $1 billion in 1939 to more than $19 billion in 1945.

To achieve his ends FDR also promoted "withholding"—forcing employers to collect federal taxes from the pay envelopes of their employees on each payday. With a surge of revenue week by week from American workers all over the nation, FDR could raise much of the money to fight the war first and fund his welfare state next.

Roosevelt had support from many politicians in his quest to increase taxes. In the congressional debate over the withholding tax, many Democrats supported the President's idea that rights came from government. On May 14, 1943, Senator Happy Chandler (D-Ky.) said, "Mr. President, all of us owe the government; we owe it for everything we have—and that is the basis of obligation—and the government can take everything we have if the government needs it." Chandler wanted to be clear on this point. "The government," he added, "can assert its right to have all the taxes it needs for any purpose, either now or at any time in the future."

To help persuade Americans during the war to accept paying taxes at higher rates, Irving Berlin, the great songwriter, produced a propaganda masterpiece entitled, "I Paid My Income Tax Today." Singer Danny Kaye recorded the song, and the Treasury sent it to 872 radio stations with a letter urging that it be played frequently. Berlin's song, which appealed to pride and patriotism, had these lyrics:

> I paid my income tax today.
> I never felt so proud before,
> To be right there with the millions more
> Who paid their income tax today.
> I'm squared up with the U.S.A.
> You see those bombers in the sky;
> Rockefeller helped to build them,
> So did I!
> I paid my income tax today.

American radio stations, which owed their licenses to the federal government, played the tax song and other tax messages from the Treasury.

Roosevelt died in 1945, before the war was won, but the tax system he favored would set the agenda for the political debate for the next two generations. The President used the war emergency to raise taxes, and his successor, Harry Truman, kept them high after the war to support FDR's Economic Bill of Rights. The debate over the federal government's role in job creation, education, housing, and medical care has shaped American politics through the present day.

> "As written, the Bill of Rights is a beneficial summary of many of the limitations that should be placed on government power."

The Bill of Rights Never Actually Limited Government Power

Ryan McMaken

In the following viewpoint, Ryan McMaken praises the Bill of Rights for protecting individual liberty from government interference. He takes issue, however, with the rest of the Constitution. Designed by "crony capitalists," McMaken says, who aimed only to aid the rich, the founding document itself is not worth celebrating. As you read, notice how difficult it is to place these viewpoints and their criticisms of the government into a typical left/right dichotomy. Ryan McMaken is an economist and the editor of Mises Wire, *a libertarian publication.*

As you read, consider the following questions:

1. Why were the Federalists willing to agree to the Bill of Rights?
2. What might have made the Bill of Rights stronger?
3. The author says that the American public tolerates routine violations of certain amendments. Which ones, and why?

"Why the Bill of Rights Is Failing," by Ryan McMaken, Mises Institute, December 15, 2016. Reprinted by permission.

T wenty-five years ago today, the first ten amendments were added to the new Constitution of 1787. Those amendments have come to be known as the Bill of Rights, and taken as a whole, these amendments represent what can only be described as one of the few parts of the Constitution worth applauding today.

While most of the Constitution is concerned with centralizing government power, raising tax revenue, protecting the institution of chattel slavery, and hammering the independent states into a consolidated political union, the Bill of Rights, on the other hand, was concerned with limiting government power:

> Bizarrely revered by many as a "pro-freedom" document, the document now generally called "the Constitution" was originally devoted almost entirely toward creating a new, bigger, more coercive, more expensive version of the United States. The United States, of course, had already existed since 1777 under a functioning constitution that had allowed the United States to enter into numerous international alliances and win a war against the most powerful empire on earth.
>
> That wasn't good enough for the oligarchs of the day, the crony capitalists with names like Washington, Madison, and, Hamilton. Hamilton and friends had long plotted for a more powerful United States government to allow the mega-rich of the time, like George Washington and James Madison, to more easily develop their lands and investments with the help of government infrastructure. Hamilton wanted to create a clone of the British empire to allow him to indulge his grandiose dreams of financial imperialism.

Fortunately, there were some who stood in the way of the people we now refer to as "the Founding Fathers." They were the anti-federalists—the good guys who stood against Washington and his friends—and who demanded a Bill of Rights before they would even consider ratifying the new Constitution.

In the end, however, the Bill of Rights was far weaker than it should have been. It was, essentially, just a bone the Federalists threw to the opposition in order to get the new Constitution ratified. The anti-Federalists, after all, couldn't even conceive of a federal government as enormous, bloated, and powerful as the US government is today. Living in a world where the individual state governments were both highly democratic and powerful in relation to the central government, the anti-Federalists figured they had enough tools at their disposal to prevent the sort of centralization that has taken place over the past two hundred years. The optimistic anti-Federalists were, unfortunately, wrong.

But, there was much more than could have been done had the anti-Federalists insisted. William Watkins offers some insights today into what could have been:

> The state conventions that ratified the Constitution suggested over 200 amendments to the Constitution to cure structural problems. For example, Virginia offered a lengthy amendment on the judicial power. The proposal, in the main, would have limited the federal judiciary to the Supreme Court and various admiralty courts established by Congress. State courts would serve as the trial courts of the Union with the possibility of appeal to the Supreme Court. Virginians rightly feared that the federal judiciary would become an engine of consolidated government and sought to limit its power.
>
> Massachusetts feared the new power of taxation in the federal government. Massachusetts, through the pen of John Hancock, offered a proposal that would have prohibited Congress from levying direct taxes … As a check on the national government, Massachusetts wanted the states to retain some control on Congress's demands for revenue.
>
> Massachusetts also proposed an amendment dealing with concerns about inadequate representation. Massachusetts asked that the Constitution be amended to guarantee "one representative to every thirty thousand persons . . . A ratio in excess of one representative for every 30,000 people would not, in Massachusetts's opinion, be a true and viable representation. How disappointed would Hancock and Company be to see that today we average 1 representative for about every 750,000 person.

Do we have truly representative government? Not in the eyes of the patriots from Massachusetts who understood that true representation can only take place on a human scale.

Rather than sitting back today and mindlessly celebrating the "high temple" of our constitutional order, Americans should dust off copies of the substantive amendments proposed by the state ratifying conventions but ignored by Madison and the Federalist majority in the first Congress. (Massachusetts' Amendments, Virginia's Amendments, New York's Amendments, North Carolina's Amendments).

The Bill of Rights Means Nothing Without the Liberal Ideology The Produced It

Better, more limiting, and more numerous amendments may indeed have been helpful.

But, no law written on parchment can control the size and scope of government if the population is willing to accept more state control over their lives.

The fact remains that the American public generally tolerates countless violations of the Tenth Amendment, the Ninth Amendment, the Sixth Amendment, the Fourth Amendment, and the Second Amendment. The federal government routinely seizes private property without due process, fails to provide for speedy trials, passes federal gun control laws, and invents powers for itself that are reserved to the states and the citizens alone. Even the First Amendment is now being targeted by the feds who are the throes of limiting freedom of speech and freedom of the press by labeling objectionable ideas as "fake news" and thus not so-called protected speech.

These attacks will be tolerated if the public is willing to go on doing so. After all, the Bill of Rights itself never actually limited government power. Government power—to the extent it has actually been limited—was limited because citizens valued the ideas reflected in the Bill of Rights.

Once the public abandons the ideology behind the Bill of Rights, then the Bill of Rights will cease to mean anything, even if it still ostensibly remains in force.

Not surprisingly, as the public ideological views have changed, the Constitution has failed to limit the power of the central government. Murray Rothbard observed this long ago when he wrote:

> From any libertarian, or even conservative, point of view, it has failed and failed abysmally; for let us never forget that every one of the despotic incursions on man's rights in this century, before, during and after the New Deal, have received the official stamp of Constitutional blessing.

Rothbard was echoing Lysander Spooner who wrote:

> But whether the Constitution really be one thing, or another, this much is certain—that it has either authorized such a government as we have had, or has been powerless to prevent it. In either case, it is unfit to exist.

From a legal standpoint, this state of affairs was easy to bring about because in practice the Constitution, including the Bill of Rights, means whatever the Supreme Court says it means. But, even the Court is limited by the public's ideological views and the public's willingness to tolerate the Court's rulings. If the public is willing to accept the seizure of private property in the name of the War on Drugs or the War on Terrorism, then we should not be surprised when government agencies do so. If the public is willing to grant the federal government powers that are clearly not found in the Constitution itself, the fact that the Bill of Rights legally prohibits such things will be of little consequence.

As written, the Bill of Rights is a beneficial summary of many of the limitations that should be placed on government power. Without a public rooted in an ideology that supports and demands respect for the Bill of Rights, however, the words will ultimately mean nothing at all.

> *"Although the framers had sought political freedom by setting up structural features to prevent the concentration of government power, the New Dealers believed they could preserve liberty strictly through the judiciary's enforcement of specified individual freedoms."*

Judicial Activism Has Weakened Constitutional Protections of Individuals

Patrick M. Garry

In the following viewpoint, Patrick M. Garry looks at the Warren Court—the years between 1953 and 1969, when Earl Warren was Chief Justice—and argues that starting with Warren's tenure, the Supreme Court has vigorously defended the rights of the individual at the expense of protecting the parts of the Constitution that would, according to this author, limit government and thus protect individual rights. Garry argues that this judicial activism has actually weakened the cause of liberty. Patrick M. Garry is a legal scholar who specializes in constitutional history.

"The Constitution's Structural Limitations on Power Should Be the Focus of the Bill of Rights," by Patrick M. Garry, Liberty Fund, Inc, January 2, 2014. Reprinted by permission.

As you read, consider the following questions:

1. According to this author, how did jurisprudence change during the years of the Warren Court?
2. When does Garry say that the Court stopped enforcing the limited government provisions of the Constitution? Why do you think that may have happened at that particular time in history?
3. How do you think this author would respond to the author in viewpoint 3 of this chapter who argues that the Constitution was designed to support the interests of only the wealthy?

Ever since the Warren era of expansive individual rights jurisprudence, leading to the Court's substantive due process jurisprudence culminating in *Roe* v. *Wade*, jurists, as well as the public at large, have grappled with the issue of judicial activism in the individual rights area. At the same time, by the time of the Warren Court, constitutional law had evolved to the point of denying the courts any meaningful role in enforcing the limited government principles incorporated in the Constitution. This essay, recognizing the continuing controversy over the Court's individual rights jurisprudence, attempts to reconcile these two different strains in constitutional development in a proposed limited government model of the Bill of Rights.

The vitriolic reaction to the fairly recent injection of limited government principles into the nation's political dialogue demonstrates how marginalized the notion of limited government has become since the 1930s. Furthermore, the widespread conviction that the Supreme Court would never strike down the Affordable Care Act on limited government principles likewise shows how unaccustomed the legal and political systems have become to judicial enforcement of those principles.[1] However, not only are limited government principles among the most important aspects of the US Constitution, but they are key to understanding the provisions in the Bill of Rights regarding individual liberty. Indeed, the decline of limited government principles during the New Deal era, combined with the rise of an individual autonomy jurisprudence during the Warren Court era, has distorted the originally-intended meaning of the Bill of Rights.

Under the leadership of Chief Justice Warren, the Court adopted an individual rights jurisprudence that interpreted the Bill of Rights as existing for the purpose of achieving a certain vision of individual autonomy. This view gained a footing during the New Deal period, when the Court retreated from enforcing the limited government structural provisions of the Constitution, such as federalism and separation of powers, while at the same time heightening its scrutiny of substantive individual rights, such as those contained in the Bill of Rights.[2] But this shift in the Court's orientation cast the Bill of Rights as concerned exclusively with individual autonomy, rather than with providing structural limitations on government power, thereby separating the Bill from the structural orientation of the Constitution as a whole. This modern view sees individual rights in isolation, as if the Constitution was primarily focused on protecting individual autonomy, not on creating a frame of government.

Under a limited government model, the Bill of Rights can be understood within the context of a larger goal—namely, ensuring the maintenance of limited government within the constitutional scheme. As the primary advocates for the Bill of Rights, the Anti-Federalists sought to achieve not particular substantive protections of a finite list of specific individual rights, but rather an assurance that the new federal government would indeed be a government of limited powers.[3] The Anti-Federalists feared that the original Constitution had not adequately prevented the new government from overstepping its allotted powers. To further secure a limited government, the Bill of Rights specified certain areas in which the government expressly had no power to act. Whereas the rest of the constitutional scheme set out structural provisions for the overall maintenance of limited government, the Bill of Rights articulated specific substantive areas in which the principle of limited government was to prevail. Nonetheless, the impetus for the Bill of Rights arose from the same limited government concerns that were incorporated in the original Constitution, and in this way the Bill of Rights is consistent with the original Constitution.

As James Madison put it, a Bill of Rights was added "for greater caution" to ensure a limited government.[4] When he introduced his proposal for a Bill of Rights in the First Congress in June of 1789, Madison explained that the purpose of this Bill was "to limit and qualify the powers of government."[5] It would provide a second limitation on the power of government. The first limitation arose from the enumerated powers doctrine, prohibited the federal government from exercising any power not explicitly granted to it by the Constitution. But the Bill of Rights placed limits on even those enumerated powers, forbidding the federal government from using its delegated powers to encroach on areas outlined by the Bill of Rights.[6] By carving out particular areas that might possibly be regulated by the government under the Necessary and Proper Clause, the Bill of Rights sets out more specific standards enabling the people to better judge whether government had exceeded its power.[7]

What is often ignored about the Bill of Rights is that it was drafted and ratified with a view toward integrating it into the overall scheme of the original Constitution, which was structural. And the most important structural aspects of the Constitution were those aimed at ensuring limited government. As a whole, the Constitution is primarily one of "powers, structures and procedures, not of values."[8]

According to Akhil Amar, the Bill of Rights is each "part of a single coherent constitution; and are reflective of a deep design; aimed at limiting government power."[9] But if consistent with the constitutional scheme and its emphasis on structure, then the Bill of Rights should not be viewed in terms of individual autonomy, but in terms of employing the language of rights to limit government power. As Gary Lawson argues, the meaning of the Bill of Rights lies primarily in the structure and history of the original Constitution, rather than in the specific wording of each of the amendments.[10]

In The Federalist, Hamilton makes a clear distinction between a free government and a republican government.[11] Whereas free government focuses on securing specified individual rights, republican government tries to achieve a more general political freedom as a means to securing individual freedom.[12] In choosing the latter, the framers saw the structure of government as the best protection of individual rights. For this reason, the Constitution's primary focus is not on providing a finite list of individual rights, but on creating structural features that protect against systemic government abuses and overreaching.[13]

But the Bill of Rights is more than just a way to generally limit the power of the federal government; the rights protected by the Bill of Rights were those that were most effective in empowering people to control and limit their government. Not only did the Bill of Rights create limitations on government, but it specifically identified areas of freedom which, when exercised, could further help to limit government. To the framers, the only real way to prevent government from violating the liberty of its citizens was to give those citizens the capacity to control government.[14] For instance, the Anti-Federalists often contended that freedom of speech and press were invaluable bulwarks against tyranny, and that exercise of those rights was necessary to control and limit government.[15] Freedoms of speech and press were seen as the essence of free government, through which people could be free to limit government by political means.[16]

Unquestionably, the framers of the Bill of Rights were very much concerned about individual freedom and natural rights. Indeed, this concern had inspired the Declaration of Independence. There is no historical dispute as to the desire of the framers for a constitutional system that protected liberty, and there is no dispute that the Bill of Rights served the goal of protecting liberty. However, the Bill of Rights tried to secure that goal through a means other than strictly a judicial protection of certain specific rights that in

Free Speech at the Borders

Unfortunately, so far, courts have refused to recognize the free speech implications of digital border searches. But we hope and expect that will change as courts are forced to weigh the increasing amount of sensitive information easily accessible on our devices and in the cloud, and the increasing frequency and scope of border searches of this information.

Without First Amendment protections at the border, the threat of self-censorship looms large. Travelers faced with the risk of border agent intrusion into such sensitive data are more prone to self-censorship when expressing themselves, when considering private membership in political groups, or when deciding whether to access certain reading or media material. This is especially true for people who belong to unpopular groups, who espouse unpopular opinions, or who read unpopular books or view unpopular movies.

Likewise, confidential sources that provide invaluable information to the public about government or corporate malfeasance may refrain from whistleblowing if they fear journalists cannot protect their identities during border crossings. This is why EFF is calling for stronger Constitutional protection of your digital information and urging people to contact Congress on this issue today.

The good news is there's a lot you can do at the border to protect your digital privacy. Take the time to review our pocket guides on Knowing Your Rights and Protecting your Digital Data at the border. And for a deeper dive into these issues, take a look at our Border Search Guide on protecting the data on your devices and in the cloud.

"The Bill of Rights at the Border: The First Amendment and the Right to Anonymous Speech," by Stephanie Lacambra, Electronic Frontier Foundation, March 22, 2017.

turn defined a particular notion of individual autonomy. Instead, limited government became the means by which liberty would be protected.

The framing generation did not know how to go about the goal of using specific constitutional provisions to protect natural rights or specific understandings of individual autonomy. They did not have a sufficiently clear idea of the parameters and scope of those individual rights. To the framers, natural or individual rights were vague and highly abstract.[17] As Philip Hamburger writes, theories of natural rights were not only so ambiguous and imprecise as to prevent broad consensus, but in fact were the subject of "substantial differences" among eighteenth-century Americans.[18] Moreover, the framers were reluctant to give the judiciary the kind of unbounded power it would need to define and enforce individual rights, so they crafted a Bill that focused not on the substance of each right but on limiting the power of government in certain areas. For instance, Madison drafted the First Amendment in the hard language of denials of government power, not in more general statements aimed at defining the nature and value of particular individual rights.[19] This language was in stark contrast to the softer kind of language in state constitutions, which focused on the moral value of liberty and individual rights and which were phrased more as obligations than as prohibitions.[20]

Furthermore, if the Bill of Rights was meant to protect fundamental or natural rights, it is curious as to why those protections were not granted vis-à-vis the states. When the Framers did seek to protect a right or freedom on its own accord, rather than as a means of limiting power, they did so in a manner that would protect that right or freedom from all governments, including state governments. The Contract Clause, for instance, specifically applies to both the federal and state governments.

Not only was the Bill of Rights not applied to the states, but the constitutional generation tolerated significant state regulation of those rights, thus further undermining the notion that the Bill served primarily to protect individual autonomy. For instance, late eighteenth century Americans accepted highly restrictive state laws on speech and press.[21]

The Ninth and Tenth Amendments in particular reflect the focus of the entire Bill of Rights as being limitations on the power of the federal government. The Tenth Amendment incorporated the rule of enumerated power, with all nondelegated power reserved to the states, whereas the Ninth Amendment limited the interpretation of the federal powers that were enumerated. As James Madison explained, the Tenth Amendment prohibited the federal government from exercising any source of power not specified within the Constitution itself, and the Ninth Amendment prohibited any interpretations of enumerated federal powers that would unduly expand federal power.[22] According to Kurt Lash, the Ninth and Tenth Amendments reflected such a universal desire for limited government that they faced very little opposition.[23]

The rise of the individual autonomy model of the Bill of Rights occurred in the wake of the New Deal demise of limited government principles. During the New Deal period, the notion of protecting liberty through the maintenance of limited and divided government gave way to the desire to ensure economic security through a powerful and activist central government. The framers' view of political freedom requiring a limited government was largely abandoned by the New Deal reformers, who called upon an activist federal government to combat the problems of the Great Depression. Although the framers had sought political freedom by setting up structural features to prevent the concentration of government power, the New Dealers believed they could preserve liberty strictly through the judiciary's enforcement of specified individual freedoms.[24]

However, this abandonment of limited government provisions undercut a fundamental protection of liberty. To compensate for this loss of constitutional protection, the Court made a compromise: although it would retreat from reviewing structural issues, it would intensify its review of substantive individual rights issues. Larry Kramer calls this the New Deal "settlement."[25]

The Warren Court era solidified the transformation in constitutional approaches to the preservation of liberty—from relying on the limited government provisions of the Constitution to focusing almost exclusively on the judicial enforcement of substantive individual rights.[26] In doing so, the Warren and Burger Courts effected a constitutional revolution in many areas of substantive individual rights. But this transformation essentially viewed the protection of individual rights as the primary purpose of constitutional law. It misinterpreted the nature of the Bill of Rights and how the Constitution went about protecting liberty. It looked on the Bill of Rights as an almost unlimited grant of power to the judiciary to enforce its view of individual autonomy, while at the same time attempting to reconcile individual liberty with a virtually unlimited federal government.

In seeking to protect liberty exclusively through judicial enforcement of specific individual substantive rights, the Court ceased protecting the kind of governmental structures designed to guard individual liberty. But when that happens, only the judiciary is left to act as the guardian of liberty—and it does so by exercising great power to define and enforce an array of specific individual substantive rights.

Notes

1. See Nat'l Fed'n of Indep. Bus. v. Sebelius, 132 S. Ct. 2566 (2012), where five Justices affirmed the limited government principles of the Constitution, specifically that Congress' commerce power is limited, even though the Court upheld the Affordable Care Act based on Congress' taxing power, and where the Court enforced federalism principles in striking down Congress' attempted expansion of Medicaid.

2. See U.S. v. Caroline Products, 304 U.S. 144, 152 n.4 (1938). For a discussion of the Court's New Deal jurisprudence, see Patrick M. Garry, An Entrenched Legacy: How the New Deal Constitutional Revolution Continues to Shape the Role of the Supreme Court102-08 (2008).

3. See Patrick M. Garry, Liberty Through Limits: The Bill of Rights as Limited Government Provisions, 62 SMU L. Rev. 1745 (2009).

4. James Madison, Speech in Congress Proposing Constitutional Amendments (June 8, 1789), in 12 The Papers of James Madison 196, 202 (Charles F. Hobson and Robert A. Rutland eds., 1979).

5. James Madison, Speech to House of Representatives (June 8, 1789), in Creating the Bill of Rights: The Documentary Record from the First Federal Congress 81 (Helen Veit et al. eds., 1991).

6. See Michael Dorf, Incidental Burdens on Fundamental Rights, 109 Harv. L. Rev. 1175, 1189 (1996).

7. Michael McConnell, Natural Rights and the Ninth Amendment, 5 N.Y.U. J.L. & Liberty 1,18 (2010); Jack Rakove, Original Meanings, 336 (1997).

8. Robert Delahunty, 1 Univ. of St. Thomas Journal of Public Law and Policy, 1, 68 (2007). In The Federalist No. 38, James Madison argued that the Bill of Rights "ought to be declaratory, not of the personal rights of individuals, but of the rights reserved to the states in their political capacity." The Federalist No. 38, at 235 (James Madison) (Clinton Rossiter, ed., 1961).

9. Akhil Reed Amar, Intratextualism, 112 Harv. L. Rev. 747, 814 (1999).

10. Gary Lawson, A Truism with Attitude: The Tenth Amendment in Constitutional Context, 83 Notre Dame L. Rev. 469, 471 (2008).

11. See, e.g., The Federalist Nos. 9, 51 (A. Hamilton) (Jacob E. Cooke ed., 1961) (referencing the distinction between free governments and republican governments).

12. Bradford P. Wilson, Separation of Powers and Judicial Review in Separation of Powers and Good Government 68 (Bradford P. Wilson & Peter W. Schramm eds,, 1994).

13. Gary Lawson, Prolegomenon to Any Future Administrative Law Course: Separation of Powers and the Transcendental Deduction, 49 St. Louis U. L.J. 885 (2005).

14. Thomas McAffee, Restoring the Lost World of Classical Legal Thought, 75 U. of Cin. L. Rev. 1499, 1572 (2007).

15. See Letters of Centinel No. 2, in 2 The Complete Anti-Federalist 143-144 (Herbert J. Storing ed. 1981); Speech of Patrick Henry in Virginia Ratifying Convention in 3 The Debates in the Several State Conventions on the Adoption of the Federal Constitution 449 (Jonathan Elliott ed., 2d Ed. 1836).

16. See James Madison, Report on the Virginia Resolutions (January 1800, reprinted in 5 The Founders' Constitution 145 (Philip B. Kurland and Ralph Lerner eds., 1987).

17. John Phillip Reid, Constitutional History of the American Revolution 10-11 (1986).

18. Philip Hamburger, Natural Rights, Natural Law and American Constitutions, 102 Yale L.J. 907, 926, 955 (1993).

19. Thomas McAffee, Inalienable Rights, Legal Enforceability, and American Constitutions, 36 Wake Forest L. Rev. 747, 777 (2001).

20. Id.

21. Hamburger, Natural Rights, 102 Yale L. J. at 911.

22. James Madison, Speech in Congress Opposing the National Bank (February 2, 1791), in James Madison, Writings 480, 481 (Jack Rakove ed., 1999).

23. Kurt Lash, James Madison's Celebrated Report of 1800, 74 Geo. Wash. L. Rev. 165, 171 (1006).

24. M.J.C. Vila, Constitutionalism and the Separation of Powers 14 (1969).

25. Larry D. Kramer, The People Themselves: Popular Constitutionalism and Judicial Review 219-20 (2004).

26. Daryl Levinson, Empire-Building Government in Constitutional Law, 118 Harv. L. Rev. 915, 971 (2005).

> "*Sometimes they get it wrong. When they do, the job of academics is to explain why the Court's answer is wrong and encourage it to do better. Instead, we have been attributing the Court's mistakes to ideological differences. We should stop.*"

The Political Climate Has Damaged the Supreme Court

Suzanna Sherry

The following viewpoint is an introduction of a symposium celebrating a book about the Supreme Court by Dean Erwin Chemerinsky, a leading constitutional scholar. The book argues that the Constitution has failed in its role of protecting the rights of minorities. In this viewpoint, Suzanna Sherry discusses Chemerinsky's thesis, and then discusses the responses to this by other members of the symposium. In the end, Sherry says that she believes that current political climate has made a politicized Court all but inevitable. Suzanna Sherry is a professor of law at Vanderbilt University.

"Introduction: Is the Supreme Court Failing at Its Job, or Are We Failing at Ours," by Suzanna Sherry, *Vanderbilt Law Review*, May 2016. Reprinted by permission.

As you read, consider the following questions:

1. What are some of the cases Chemerinsky uses to support his claim that the Supreme Court has failed to protect the rights of minorities?
2. How, according to Sherry, have academics made the problem worse, and how might they make it better?
3. Does the author conclude that justices can be totally objective politically when doing their jobs?

It is a pleasure and a privilege to write an introduction to this Symposium celebrating Dean Erwin Chemerinsky's important new book, *The Case Against the Supreme Court.*[1] Chemerinsky is one of the leading constitutional scholars of our time and a frequent advocate before the US Supreme Court. If he thinks there is a case to be made against the Court, we should all take it very seriously indeed.

Chemerinsky's thesis may be stated in a few sentences. The primary role of the Supreme Court, in his view, is to "protect the rights of minorities who cannot rely on the political process and to uphold the Constitution in the face of any repressive desires of political majorities."[2] Canvassing the Court's performance over two centuries, he concludes, first, that it has failed dismally at those tasks. Nevertheless, he reaches two additional conclusions: he believes that we can and should expect the Court to do better, and he outlines reforms that might help it do so.

Chemerinsky makes a strong case that the Court has historically failed to live up to its role. His primary historical examples—from *Dred Scott v. Sanford* and *Plessy v. Ferguson* to *Buck v. Bell* and *Korematsu v. US*—are widely thought of as reprehensible. (His contemporary examples are more controversial, as Professor Brian Fitzpatrick's contribution to the Symposium illustrates,[3] but Chemerinsky really doesn't need those examples to support his conclusions.) Where there is room for argument is on his second and third conclusions: Is it reasonable to expect the Court to live up to Chemerinsky's expectations, and how can we help ensure that it does so?

In the pages that follow, constitutional scholars address these questions. Professors Gerald Rosenberg and Corinna Lain argue that it is unrealistic to expect the Court to escape political, cultural, and structural constraints to rein in repressive popular majorities. "[T]he Supreme Court is structurally and inherently conservative,"[4] writes Rosenberg, and "the practice of judicial review has done more harm than good to those lacking power and privilege."[5] Lain argues, similarly, that the Court is ill-equipped to play the "heroic, countermajoritarian role" that Chemerinsky expects of it.[6] This is especially true in the cases that make up Chemerinsky's evidence of failure. As Lain puts it, "history shows that when minorities are most vulnerable—when society is itself repressive—the Justices are least likely to see the need to protect."[7] Or as Rosenberg says, "what [the Court] cannot do is to protect the vulnerable when the broader society is unwilling to do so."[8]

Professors Ed Rubin and Barry Friedman take the opposite position. Agreeing with Chemerinsky, they believe that the Court can and should fulfill its rights-protecting role even in repressive times. Rubin contends that even in 1927, when *Buck* v. *Bell* was decided, the Justices should have been aware that sterilization was morally reprehensible, politically controversial, and scientifically questionable.[9] The same Court that was vigorously protecting property rights in cases like *Lochner* v. *New York,* he argues, should have been more sensitive to rights of bodily integrity. Friedman has less to say about the historical examples, but agrees with Chemerinsky's condemnation of the Court for modern immunity doctrines that allow government officials to violate constitutional rights with impunity.[10] As Friedman tells the Court: "You had one job."[11] Remedying violations of rights was that one job, but immunity doctrines mean that instead of actually deciding whether rights were violated—instead of "actually call[ing] . . . balls and strikes"—the Court "defer[s] to the players themselves every time something really troubling crosses [its] plate."[12]

Chemerinsky responds to Lain and Rosenberg with two points. The first is to suggest that the question of whether the Court should have been expected to do better is "far less important to [his] project"[13] than is persuading his readers that the Court has failed, because he is not interested in "moral blameworthiness."[14] The second—somewhat in tension with the first—is to label the socio-political context of lamentable decisions "an explanation, not an excuse" and to conclude that in these decisions "the Court abandoned the underlying values of the Constitution."[15]

But persuading his readers that the Court has failed—that it has abandoned constitutional values—is the easy part. The hard part is whether (and how) we can fix the problem. And here the battle lines are drawn differently: It is Rosenberg against all the others. Even Lain, who finds the historical mistakes all but inevitable given their context, sees a silver lining.

Rosenberg, true nonbeliever that he is, holds out no hope for the Court. The subtitle of his essay says it all: Chemerinsky's suggestions for reform are nothing but "romantic longings for a mythical Court." The core of the problem, according to Rosenberg, is judicial review itself, which will always have the effect of "protect[ing] property and privilege against attempts to regulate them."[16] And the solution is to reduce the role of the Court: Keep judicial review but "vest[ ] appellate power over decisions invalidating state and federal laws in Congress."[17] Readers will draw their own conclusions, but for me, Rosenberg's proposal is terrifying. What on earth does he think the current Republican-controlled, Tea-Party-dominated Congress would do with—or to—*Roe* v. *Wade*, *Obergefell* v. *Hodges*, *Boumediene* v. *Bush*, and dozens of other cases protecting individual rights from repressive majorities? As Chemerinsky puts it, "Congress operates in [the] same political context [as the Court] and is even more likely to be responsive to it because its members have to seek reelection."[18]

So we come to the most difficult and important question: How can we reduce the probability of the Court creating today's versions of Korematsu and its ilk? *The Case Against the Supreme Court* offers numerous suggestions, the most prominent of which is to limit Supreme Court Justices to non-renewable 18-year terms.[19] Chemerinsky is not the only proponent of term limits. Rosenberg says imposing term limits is "supported by data, experience, and the findings of the branch relations literature" and "makes sense."[20] Similar proposals have been endorsed by others on both the left and the right.[21]

Whether or not term limits are a good idea in the abstract, however, they are unlikely to solve the particular problem that troubles Chemerinsky: judicial abdication of the Court's role in protecting individual rights. To the extent that the Court's failure lies in its refusal to correct majority tyranny, term-limited Justices are less likely to override majority preferences. First, a Court made up of Justices all chosen within the past eighteen years (and half chosen within the decade) is more rather than less likely to agree with contemporary popular sentiments. Repressive times will breed repressive Justices, without the potential tempering effect of colleagues from an earlier generation. Second, a term-limited Justice will have to do something after her term expires, and affiliating herself with unpopular views by protecting individual rights will limit her options.

Chemerinsky's obvious response is that part of the problem is the Justices' enforcement of property rights and states' rights—in other words, that the Court not only refuses to invalidate trespasses on individual rights, it also harms the politically vulnerable by striking legislation meant to help them.[22] On this account, the longevity of the Justices can produce what Rosenberg calls "judicial obstinance in the face of political change."[23] That's a fine argument for liberals, but not as persuasive to those who believe that property rights or states' rights are important constitutional values. As Chemerinsky himself says, there was always a danger that *The Case Against the Supreme Court* might be perceived as liberal whining, and he therefore set out "to make a case against the Supreme Court that those all across the political spectrum can accept."[24] To do so, however, he has to abandon his claim that cases like Lochner or *Hammer* v. *Dagenhart*—to say nothing of Citizens United or Shelby County—are evidence of the Court's failure. He has to rest, in other words, on universally condemned cases like *Plessy, Buck,* and *Korematsu.*[25] And those cases all involved judicial failures to act,[26] more likely to be exacerbated than alleviated by term limits.

The other participants in the Symposium offer some intriguing approaches to the problem of the Court's failures. Lain turns failure into success by suggesting that although we cannot expect the Court to be heroic, it can—and does—still do a lot of good. First, as she argues elsewhere, to the extent that legislative outcomes are not necessarily reflective of majoritarian views, the same impediments that prevent the Court from fulfilling its role as countermajoritarian savior may render it a more promising channel of progressive majoritarian change.[27] Second, she argues that the Court created its own image as guarantor of individual rights and protector of vulnerable minorities—and that expectation can in turn create "a cadre of believers" who will keep pushing boundaries until the cultural constraints ease and the expectation becomes a reality.[28]

A more indirect suggestion comes from Professor Neal Devins. He analyzes the abortion cases to illustrate the effect of political context on the success of minimalist (non-heroic) or maximalist (heroic) Supreme Court decisions.[29] His analysis is independently interesting and also shows us how the Court can take political context into account in a positive and productive way. Minimalist decisions work best, he argues, when there is a possibility of political dialogue and compromise. When dialogue and compromise are impossible because of political conditions, however, the Court should issue maximalist decisions that settle the issue. Thus, Devins suggests, *Roe* v. *Wade* was wrong for its time: There was no hard-and-fast partisan divide on abortion, and compromise was possible—and indeed occurred despite Roe—and so the Court should have issued a minimalist decision incorporating an indeterminate standard. Casey, on the other hand, was right for its time: Compromise and political discourse were still alive and well in 1992, and Casey's minimalism allowed both to flourish. Devins shows that beginning in 2010, however, political polarization has made both dialogue and compromise impossible, and thus he urges the Court to issue another maximalist decision, in other words, to "assume the heroic role" that Chemerinsky embraces.[30]

Devins's suggestion won't always solve the problem: A Court so enmeshed in contemporary mores that it cannot see its way out of them, as Lain and Rosenberg suggest happened in cases like *Buck* and *Korematsu*, will not issue maximalist rights-protective decisions. Nevertheless, it is a thoughtful approach to the problem that Chemerinsky identifies.

Friedman offers a different sort of solution to what he calls the "loss of faith" on both the right and the left.[31] He urges the Court to be more institutionally transparent: cameras in the courtroom, more information available online, shorter and clearer opinions, no more issuing all the controversial opinions at the very end of the Term. Unfortunately, none of these things are likely to satisfy critics—like Chemerinsky—who think that the true problem is that the Court is failing at its job of protecting rights.

Indeed, Friedman's suggestions are actually addressed to a different problem, which he identifies: The public has lost faith that the Court is "up to anything other than simple . . . politics."[32] Chemerinsky's book is merely Exhibit 1 in establishing the case against the Supreme Court. According to Friedman (and I agree), Chemerinsky is just one of many, on the left and the right, who are frustrated because they see the Justices as "ideological and result-oriented rather than reasoned lawgivers."[33] Pundits, politicians, and scholars have now become convinced that any decision with which they disagree must be based on ideology. As Friedman puts it, "all of a sudden everyone seemed to think the umpire was playing for some team—even if they could not say exactly which one."[34]

While Chemerinsky faults the Court for not protecting individual rights, then, Friedman cuts through that lament to what he sees as the underlying issue. Chemerinsky (and others on the left) believe that the Justices wrongly turn their conservative political preferences into constitutional law. As Friedman notes, of course, there are many on the right who think the current Court is doing just the opposite, constitutionalizing liberal political views. Hence the "loss of faith" on both sides of the aisle.

And therein lies the real failure, and it is not primarily the Court's. It is ours. Academics, especially legal academics, are in the best position to educate the public—both directly and, through the media, indirectly—about the Court and its role. If we describe the Court as politically motivated, that view is bound to seep into public consciousness sooner or later. Unfortunately, that is exactly how two quite different groups of influential legal academics have characterized the Court (and judicial decision-making generally) for the last several decades.

As early as the 1960s, prominent attitudinalist political scientists argued that judicial decisions are determined primarily by the judge's politics, and very little by legal principles.[35] Legal academics used to take issue with that claim, but lately many have been implicitly or explicitly accepting it. From popular constitutionalism[36] to Friedman's magnum opus on how the Court follows public opinion[37] and Rosenberg's insistence that expecting it to do otherwise is a hollow hope,[38] too many legal academics have bought the attitudinalist party line. It doesn't help that many liberal friends of the Warren Court—like Chemerinsky himself—have lately turned against the Court, and some conservative critics of the Warren Court have developed a previously undiscovered fondness for judicial activism. Such blatantly political reversals lend support to the conclusion that the Court itself must be political.

Beginning in the 1980s, another group of legal academics adopted a post-modern approach, arguing that knowledge and reality are social constructs made by those in power.[39] Judicial decision- making, on this theory, is simply an exercise of political power. Although the strongest form of social constructionism has largely faded from legal scholarship, the mistrust of those in positions of power—including the Supreme Court—took its toll.

Now these dangerous misconceptions about what it is that judges do in constitutional cases have reached the general public. No wonder there is a crisis of faith. Attitudinalism and post-modernism, watered down into a democracy-based critique of judicial decision- making as ideologically motivated, must take much of the blame. (To be fair, one can also blame the late Justice Scalia, whose intemperate attacks on his colleagues, such as the characterization of a recent decision as "a naked judicial claim to legislative—indeed, super-legislative—power"[40] and a "judicial Putsch,"[41] reinforced the notion that the Court is a purely political body.)

Make no mistake, however, these are misconceptions. The Court was never an umpire, calling balls and strikes, but neither are the Justices members of political "teams" or legislators in robes who do their best to enshrine their policy preferences into law. Judging necessarily involves discretion but it is neither unconstrained nor primarily political. A diverse array of internal and external safeguards—from professional norms to the demands of collaboration and opinion-writing—serves to cabin judicial discretion and channel personal preferences into principled decision-making.[42]

What Justices do in constitutional cases, in other words, is not far removed from what they do in non-constitutional cases: they look to text (if there is one), precedent, history, institutional considerations, consequences, policy concerns, and common sense to reach the best answer they can. Sometimes they get it wrong. When they do, the job of academics is to explain why the Court's answer is wrong and encourage it to do better. Instead, we have been attributing the Court's mistakes to ideological differences. We should stop.

Chemerinsky has it half right, then. The Supreme Court can do better, and we should urge it to do so. But the institutional changes he suggests are unlikely to succeed. Moreover, his use of controversial conservative decisions as contemporary examples of the Court's broader failures exacerbates the problem by politicizing judicial decision-making.

In short, if we want the Court to live up to its role as a protector of rights, we have to revive an older view of judging as reasoned decision-making based on legal principles rather than as mere political fiat.

That revival may, in the end, be impossible. As I write this, Republican senators are adamantly refusing to vote on (or, in some cases, even to meet with) President Obama's nominee for the Supreme Court—a political moderate whom some of them have previously urged as a potential nominee. A public official was willing to go to jail rather than obey a Supreme Court decision. Political polarization among both politicians and the general public is at an all-time high, and one scholar has suggested that continued polarization is inevitable in a mature democracy.[43]

In such an atmosphere, it is probably foolish to expect anyone to believe that Supreme Court Justices are capable of putting their politics aside. Certainly none of the participants in this Symposium are naive enough to believe it. So although it is indeed a pleasure and a privilege to write this introduction, one part of me mourns Chemerinsky's book and the responses to it as further evidence that we have irretrievably lost our innocence.

Notes

1. ERWIN CHEMERINSKY, THE CASE AGAINST THE SUPREME COURT (2014).

2. Id. at 10.

3. Brian Fitzpatrick, A Tribute to Justice Scalia: Why Bad Cases Make Bad Methodology, 69 VAND. L. REV. 991 (2016).

4. Gerald N. Rosenberg, The Broken-Hearted Lover: Erwin Chemerinsky's Romantic Longings for a Mythical Court, 69 VAND. L. REV. 1075, 1078 (2016).

5. Id. at 1111.

6. Corinna Barrett Lain, Three Supreme Court "Failures" and a Story of Supreme Court Success, 69 VAND. L. REV. 1019, 1022–23 (2016).

7. Id.

8. Rosenberg, supra note 4, at 1111.

9. Edward L. Rubin, The Supreme Court in Context: Conceptual, Pragmatic, and Institutional, 69 VAND. L. REV. 1115 (2016).

10. CHEMERINSKY, supra note 1, at 197–225.

11. Barry Friedman, Letter to Supreme Court (Erwin Chemerinsky is Mad. Why You Should Care.), 69 VAND. L. REV. 995, 1015 (2016).

12. Id. at 1017. As Chemerinsky points out in his response, Friedman has previously taken a somewhat different view, suggesting that public opinion exerts a powerful influence on the Court. Erwin Chemerinsky, Thinking About the Supreme Court's Successes and Failures, 69 VAND. L. REV. 919, 927 (2016).

13. Chemerinsky, supra note 12, at 928.

14. Id. at 929.

15. Id. at 928. The tension lies in the fact that it is hard to characterize the abandonment of constitutional values as not morally blameworthy.

16. Rosenberg, supra note 4, at 1079.

17. Id. at 1112.

18. Chemerinsky, supra note 12, at 931.

19. As Rosenberg points out, none of Chemerinsky's other proposals are likely to do much good. Rosenberg, supra note 4, at 1104–12.

20. Id. at 1109.

21. See, e.g., SANFORD LEVINSON, OUR UNDEMOCRATIC CONSTITUTION 123–39 (2006); REFORMING THE COURT: TERM LIMITS FOR SUPREME COURT JUSTICES (Roger C. Cramton & Paul D. Carrington eds., 2005).

22. CHEMERINSKY, supra note 1, at 90–110.

23. Rosenberg, supra note 4, at 1110.

24. CHEMERINSKY, supra note 1, at 333–34.

25. Or even on modern cases like Hui v. Castaneda, 559 U.S. 799 (2010), and Van de Kamp v. Goldstein, 555 U.S. 335 (2009), for which Friedman takes the Court to task by suggesting that everyone can agree that they are wrong. Friedman, supra note 11, at 1015–17.

26. Dred Scott is the lone exception. See generally, Suzanna Sherry, Why We Need More Judicial Activism, in CONSTITUTIONALISM, EXECUTIVE POWER, AND THE SPIRIT OF MODERATION (Giorgi Areshidze, Paul Carrese, & Suzanna Sherry eds., forthcoming 2016), http://ssrn.com/abstract=2213372 [https://perma.cc/3DJF-NEDS] (listing universally condemned decisions and suggesting that the vast majority involve judicial failures to act).

27. Corinna Barrett Lain, Upside-Down Judicial Review, 101 GEO. L.J. 113 (2012).

28. Lain, supra note 6, at 1072-73.

29. Neal Devins, Rethinking Judicial Minimalism: Abortion Politics, Party Polarization, and the Consequences of Returning the Constitution to Elected Government, 69 VAND. L. REV. 935 (2016).

30. Id. at 936.

31. Friedman, supra note 11, at 1005.

32. Id.

33. Id. at 997.

34. Id. at 1006.

35. See, e.g., DAVID W. ROHDE & HAROLD J. SPAETH, SUPREME COURT DECISION MAKING (1976); GLENDON SCHUBERT, THE JUDICIAL MIND: THE ATTITUDES AND IDEOLOGIES OF SUPREME COURT JUSTICES, 1946-1963 (1965); JEFFREY A. SEGAL & HAROLD J. SPAETH, THE SUPREME COURT AND THE ATTITUDINAL MODEL REVISITED (2002).

36. See, e.g., LARRY D. KRAMER, THE PEOPLE THEMSELVES: POPULAR CONSTITUTIONALISM AND JUDICIAL REVIEW (2004); RICHARD D. PARKER, "HERE, THE PEOPLE RULE": A CONSTITUTIONAL POPULIST MANIFESTO (1994); JAMIN B. RASKIN, OVERRULING DEMOCRACY: THE SUPREME COURT VS. THE AMERICAN PEOPLE (2003); MARK TUSHNET, TAKING THE CONSTITUTION AWAY FROM THE COURTS (1999).

37. BARRY FRIEDMAN, THE WILL OF THE PEOPLE: HOW PUBLIC OPINION HAS INFLUENCED THE SUPREME COURT AND THE MEANING OF THE CONSTITUTION (2009).

38. See GERALD N. ROSENBERG, THE HOLLOW HOPE: CAN COURTS BRING ABOUT SOCIAL CHANGE? (2d ed. 2008).

39. For a description and critique of this approach, see DANIEL A. FARBER & SUZANNA SHERRY, BEYOND ALL REASON: THE RADICAL ASSAULT ON TRUTH IN AMERICAN LAW (1997).

40. Obergefell v. Hodges, 135 S. Ct. 2584, 2629 (2015) (Scalia, J., dissenting).

41. Id.

42. For elaborations of this argument, see DANIEL A. FARBER & SUZANNA SHERRY, JUDGMENT CALLS: PRINCIPLE AND POLITICS IN CONSTITUTIONAL LAW (2009); Suzanna Sherry, Politics and Judgment, 70 MO. L. REV. 973 (2005).

43. See Richard H. Pildes, Why the Center Does Not Hold: The Causes of Hyperpolarized Democracy in America, 99 CALIF. L. REV. 273 (2011).

Periodical and Internet Sources Bibliography

The following articles have been selected to supplement the diverse views presented in this chapter.

Yoni Applebaum, "American's Fragile Constitution," *Atlantic*, December 12, 2017. https://www.theatlantic.com/magazine/archive/2015/10/our-fragile-constitution/403237/.

Emily Cadei, "Going 'Nuclear' on Gorsuch Promises More Politicized Courts," *Newsweek*, April 7, 2017. http://www.newsweek.com/filibuster-gorsuch-judicial-branch-580578.

Joel Cohen, Richard Posner, and Jed Rakoff, "Should Judges Use Their Roles to Effect Social Change?: A Dialogue about Whether 'Activist" Judges Are Real" *Slate*, August 24, 2017. http://www.slate.com/articles/news_and_politics/jurisprudence/2017/08/posner_rakoff_dialogue_on_how_judges_should_effect_social_changes.html.

David French, "The Supreme Court Is a Dangerous Conservative Obsession," *National Review*, November 21, 2017. http://www.nationalreview.com/article/453969/conservatives-supreme-court-obsession-dangerous.

James W. Lucas, "The Supreme Court versus the Constitution," *National Review*, December 8, 2017. http://www.nationalreview.com/article/454464/constitutional-amendment-simplify-procedure.

Nick Perry, "Roberts Says Supreme Court Confirmation Process Too Politicized," *Bloomberg Politics*, July 26, 2017. https://www.bloomberg.com/news/articles/2017-07-26/chief-justice-roberts-technology-poses-challenge-for-court.

Jedediah Purdy, "Scalia's Contradictory Originalism," *The New Yorker*, February 16, 2016. https://www.newyorker.com/news/news-desk/scalias-contradictory-originalism.

Cass Sunstein, "Gorsuch's Rejection of a Politicized Executive Branch," *Bloomberg Review*, October 2, 2017. https://www.bloomberg.com/view/articles/2017-10-02/gorsuch-s-rejection-of-a-politicized-executive-branch.

For Further Discussion

Chapter 1

1. What were the arguments made for and against the inclusion of a Bill of Rights in the US Constitution? How might the history of the country have been different if those who were opposed had prevailed?
2. What are some of the informal methods of changing the Constitution mentioned in this chapter? Can you think of other examples of how informal changes might happen now or in the near future?
3. Do you think there is a need for an amendment guaranteeing the right to vote. Why or why not?

Chapter 2

1. People often see the varying philosophies of judicial interpretation as a partisan issue. After reading the viewpoints in this chapter, do you agree?
2. Those who see the Constitution as a "living document," subject to interpretations that change throughout history, are often accused of making the Constitution into anything they want it to be. Do you think this is true? What do you think might be the consequences of too-fluid an interpretation? Of too strict an interpretation?
3. What are some ways that eighteenth-century America was fundamentally different from modern America? Should we take those differences into account when interpreting the Constitution? If not, can you imagine what the results might be?

Chapter 3

1. The Supreme Court decision *Marbury* v. *Madison* gave the Court the right to invalidate laws that were not consistent with the Constitution. Did this in and of itself give the court too much power to affect law?

2. Everyone agrees that the role of the court is to be a check on the power of the other branches. Do you think that activist judges are abusing that power? Do you think that a commitment to judicial restraint can lead to an abdication of that power?

3. In this chapter, Evan Bernick argues that judges should examine the intent of legislators when making their rulings. Do you agree? What do you think Bernick really means by "judicial engagement"? Do you think he makes that clear in his essay?

Chapter 4

1. In today's society, the role of the court comes up very often in political discussions, elections, and so on. Do you think the court has become too politicized? If so, can you think of ways to reverse that trend?

2. What changes to the course of history would have occurred if the anti-Federalists' proposed Constitutional amendments had been made?

3. Do you think the politicization of the Supreme Court has harmed the United States? Why or why not?

Organizations to Contact

The editors have compiled the following list of organizations concerned with the issues debated in this book. The descriptions are derived from materials provided by the organizations. All have publications or information available for interested readers. The list was compiled on the date of publication of the present volume; the information provided here may change. Be aware that many organizations take several weeks or longer to respond to inquiries, so allow as much time as possible.

American Civil Liberties Union (ACLU)

125 Broad Street, 18th Floor, New York, NY 10001
(212) 549-2500
website: www.aclu.org

The ACLU is an organization that works, via litigation and lobbying, to defend and protect the individual rights and liberties that are guaranteed by the Constitution of the United States. It was founded in 1920 with an emphasis primarily on freedom of speech for war protestors, but has since expanded to protect other groups and other rights.

American Constitution Society for Law and Policy

1333 H St, NW, 11th Floor
Washington, DC 20005
(202) 393-6181
email: info@ACSLaw.org
website: www.acslaw.org

The American Constitution Society for Law and Policy is a progressive organization that brings together the country's best legal minds to help shape progressive vision of the Constitution. It focuses on access to justice, voting rights, and health care reform among other issues.

Bill of Rights Institute

1310 North Courthouse Road #620
Arlington, VA 22201
(703) 894-1776
email : Info@billofrightsinstitute.org
website : www.billofrightsinstitute.org

The Bill of Rights Institute is an organization devoted to presenting to schoolchildren a conservative interpretation of the Constitution. It provides lesson plans, resources, and seminars for teachers, and contests, games, and leadership seminars for students.

Brennan Center for Justice

120 Broadway
Suite 1750
New York, NY 10271
(646) 292-8310
email: brennancenter@nyu.edu
website: www.brennancenter.org

This nonpartisan law and policy institute works to hold the United States to its promises of democracy and equal justice for all, including efforts to protect voting rights. Issues include voting rights, campaign finance reform, and protection of rights in the fight against terrorism.

Canadian Civil Liberties Association

9 Eglinton Ave E
Toronto, ON M4P 2Y3
(416) 363-0321
email: mail@ccla.org
website: www.ccla.org

The Canadian Civil Liberties Association is an organization fighting for the civil liberties, human rights, and democratic freedoms of people all across

Canada. It focuses on issues of equality, national security, fundamental freedoms, and public safety.

Cato Institute/Center for Constitutional Studies

1000 Massachusetts Ave, NW
Washington, DC 20001-5403
(202)842-0200
website: www.cato.org/research/constitutional-studies

The Center for Constitutional studies is a Libertarian organization dedicated to promoting a narrow reading of the Constitution. The Cato Institute is a think tank that supports limited government, free markets, and peace. It is dedicated to the idea that economic as well as social freedom is necessary for a free society, and works to educate the public about its views.

Center for Constitutional Rights

666 Broadway
7th Floor
New York, NY 10012
(212) 614-6464
website: https://ccrjustice.org

The Center for Constitutional Rights is a progressive organization working to protect the rights guaranteed by the Constitution and promote social justice. It used advocacy and creative legal strategies to end LBGTQ persecution, racial injustice, abusive immigration practices, and the criminalization of dissent.

Constitutional Accountability Center

1200 18th Street NW
Suite 501
Washington, DC 20036
(202) 296-6889
website: www.theusconstitution.org

The Constitutional Accountability Center is a think tank dedicated to fulfilling the progressive promise of the Constitution's history. The CAC believes that the best approach to Constitutional interpretation lies between the extremes of originalism advocated by Justice Scalia and the idea that the text of the Constitution does not provide answers.

The Constitution Project

1200 18th Street, NW Suite 1000 Washington DC, 20036
202-580-6920
email: info@constitutionproject.org
website: www.constitutionproject.org

This organization works to address the partisan divide in the interpretation of the Constitution. It works to protect the rule of law against excessive presidential authority, and to protect the checks and balances established in the Constitution.

Constitutional Rights Foundation

601 S. Kingsley Dr.
Los Angeles, CA 90005
(213) 487-5590
website: www.Crf-usa.org

The Constitutional Rights Foundation is an organization that seeks to instill in young people an appreciation for the Constitution and the Bill of Rights. This community-based organization provides resources for student and teachers, and offers online lessons about civics and the Bill of Rights.

Bibliography of Books

Akhil Reed Amar. *America's Constitution: A Biography.* New York, NY: Random House, 2005.

Carol Berkin. *The Bill of Rights: The Fight to Secure America's Liberties.* New York, NY: Simon and Schuster, 2016.

Mary Sarah Bilder. *Madison's Hand: Revising the Constitutional Convention.* Cambridge, MA: Harvard University Press, 2015.

Erwin Cherminsky. *The Case Against the Supreme Court.* New York, NY: Penguin, 2014.

Ralph Ketcham, ed. *The Anti-Federalist Papers.* New York, NY: Signet Classics, 1986.

Michael J. Klarman. *The Framers' Coup: the Making of the United States Constitution.* Oxford, UK: Oxford University Press, 2016.

Ian Millhiser. *Injustices: The Supreme Court's History of Comforting the Comfortable and Afflicting the Afflicted.* New York, NY: Nation Books, 2015.

Linda R. Monk. *The Bill of Rights: A User's Guide.* New York, NY: Hachette, 2018.

Steve Pincus. *The Heart of the Declaration: The Founders' Case for an Activist Government.* New Haven, CT: Yale University Press, 2016.

David Brian Robertson. *The Original Compromise: What the Constitutions' Framers Were Really Thinking.* Oxford, UK: Oxford University Press, 2013.

Antonin Scalia and Bryan A. Garner. *Reading Law: The Interpretation of Legal Texts.* Eagan, MN: Thomson/West, 2012.

Antonin Scalia. *Scalia's Court: A Legacy of Opinions and Dissent.* Washington, DC: Regenery, 2016.

Shlomo Slonim. *Forging the American Nation, 1787–1791: James Madison and the Federalist Revolution.* New York, NY: Palgrave McMillan, 2017.

Juan Williams. *We the People: the Modern Day Figures Who Have Reshaped and Affirmed the Founding Fathers' Vision of America.* New York, NY: Random, 2016.

Index